"This is one of the best guidebooks for fundraising for any industry. Morrie Warshawski's approach parallels the development of a strategic business plan. Based on my experience, that's what public and private foundations demand. By following the pragmatic and systematic approach that Morrie offers, a creativity-oriented filmmaker can present the professional grant application that virtually guarantees success."

– Ernie Stewart
Executive Director
Media Communications
Association-International

"This new edition of *Shaking the Money Tree* is an invaluable and definitive resource for filmmakers at any stage in their careers, with up-to-date information, practical advice, and inside perspectives – all provided through the lens of a fundraising pro whose understanding of the particulars of media fundraising make this a resource like no other."

– Sally Jo Fifer
Executive Director
Independent Television Service (ITVS)

"A cross between a fundraising encyclopedia and a filmmaker's bible, *Shaking the Money Tree* is the ultimate source for learning everything you'll ever need to know about getting grants and donations for your film and video projects. Morrie Warshawski has written the classic text to help and inspire independent media makers grow their projects from seedlings to evergreens."

– Alan Berliner
Independent Filmmaker

"This is the best proposal guide for indie filmmakers. It covers all the essentials in easy to understand text. A must for raising money."

– Gail Silva
Executive Director
Film Arts Foundation

"Warshawski's book is an indispensable guide to understanding the world of non-profit funding. It should be required reading for every documentary filmmaker."

– Louise Levison
Author of *Filmmakers and Financing: Business Plans for Independents*

"If you are going to raise funds, you need a well thought out plan. Novices often waste time and resources learning by trial and error. In *Shaking The Money Tree*, Morrie Warshawski offers expert and no-nonsense advice that will be invaluable to filmmakers seeking grants and donations."

– Mark Litwak
Author and Entertainment Attorney

"Like it or not, money is the rocket fuel that propels every movie project forward. Morrie Warshawski has created a financial map to the stars by telling you how, when, and where you should prepare to launch your project and when to fire each stage's booster rockets besides. You may not get off the ground without it!"

– Larry Sivitz
Seattle Magazine

"Warchawski's book carefully outlines every step toward a decent budget to support the filmmaker's vision. It's an indispensable guide to success in film financing."

– Mary J. Schirmer
Award-Winning
Screenwriter/Instructor
www.screenplayers.net
www.absolutewrite.com

MICHAEL WIESE PRODUCTIONS
www.mwp.com

Since 1981, Michael Wiese Productions has been dedicated to providing novice and seasoned filmmakers with vital information on all aspects of filmmaking and videomaking. We have published more than 60 books, used in over 500 film schools worldwide.

Our authors are successful industry professionals − they believe that the more knowledge and experience they share with others, the more high-quality films will be made. That's why they spend countless hours writing about the hard stuff: budgeting, financing, directing, marketing, and distribution. Many of our authors, including myself, are often invited to conduct filmmaking seminars around the world.

We truly hope that our publications, seminars, and consulting services will empower you to create enduring films that will last for generations to come.

We're here to help. Let us hear from you.

Sincerely,

Michael Wiese
Publisher, Filmmaker

SHAKING THE MONEY TREE

HOW TO GET GRANTS AND

DONATIONS FOR FILM AND VIDEO PROJECTS

2ND EDITION

MORRIE WARSHAWSKI

Published by Michael Wiese Productions
11288 Ventura Blvd., Suite 621
Studio City, CA 91604
tel. (818) 379-8799
fax (818) 986-3408
mw@mwp.com
www.mwp.com

Cover Design: Murdock Advertising & Design
Book Layout: Gina Mansfield
Editor: Brett Jay Markel

Printed by McNaughton & Gunn, Inc., Saline, Michigan
Manufactured in the United States of America

Library of Congress Cataloging-in-Publication Data

Warshawski, Morrie.
  Shaking the money tree : how to get grants and donations for film and video projects / Morrie Warshawski.-- 2nd ed.
       p. cm.
   ISBN 0-941188-79-5
1. Motion picture industry--United States--Finance. 2. Video recording--United States--Finance. I. Title.
   PN1993.5.U6W33 2003
   384'.83'0973--dc21
                                    2003005857

DEDICATED TO

EVY, LEAH, AND MAURA

MY THREE MUSES

"Until one is committed, there is hesitance, the chance to draw back, always ineffectiveness. Concerning all acts of initiative (and creation) there is one elementary truth, the ignorance of which kills countless ideas and splendid plans: that the moment one definitely commits oneself, then Providence moves, too.

All sorts of things occur to help one that would never have otherwise occurred. A whole stream of events issues from the decision, raising in one's favour all manner of unforeseen incidents, meetings, and material assistance, which no man would have dreamed could have come his way.

Whatever you can do or dream you can, begin it. Boldness has genius, power and magic in it. Begin it now."

— Goethe, German Poet/Dramatist, 1749-1832

INTRODUCTION

When I approached Michael Wiese with the idea for the first edition of this book in 1993, I had only one goal in mind: to create a text that would empower independent film and video artists to find grants and donations on their own. Filmmakers were bombarding me with questions and queries about fundraising for their projects – usually in a desperate attempt to find that last chunk of support needed for post-production, or at a moment when they had "hit the wall" and could not understand why everyone was saying "no" to their proposals.

I set out to create a text that was readable, easy to understand, and that demystified the entire process of fundraising for film; a book that would give the filmmaker the tools necessary to conduct a smart and successful fundraising campaign without having to call me up and pay a lot of money for consulting support. The book first appeared in 1994 and quickly went into three printings. Since its appearance I have received letters, phone calls, and e-mails from filmmakers all over the world expressing their thanks for bits of advice in the book that helped them find money for their projects.

And, since the book went out of print a couple of years ago, I have also received many requests for a brand new edition. Apparently dog-eared copies make the rounds from hand-to-hand, and the book is often stolen (especially from libraries) and never returned. Recently, when Michael Wiese approached me about creating a completely new edition, I realized that the time was right and the field was ready.

I believe in creating works that are as "evergreen" as possible – that can withstand the test of time and do not become outdated as soon as they hit the streets. In this edition, as in my first, the emphasis is on advice that will hold true for some time to come. The basic principles of effective fundraising are not about to change in the near future –

filmmakers will always need to learn how to comport themselves properly, configure their projects powerfully and carefully, and how to research and personalize all proposals. These are basic bottom line algorithms of funding that time will not alter.

Even so, the larger environment surrounding fundraising will continue to be in flux. The most dramatic development since my first edition has been the advent of the Internet. It may be difficult to believe, but in my first edition the Web and e-mail played absolutely no role at all in fundraising! Now, use of the Internet is a key component in doing research, maintaining contact with funders, and creating an effective marketing campaign. Another moving target is the economy. When the economy is in decline, it is typical that foundation coffers decrease and corporate donations diminish. The dramatic change here since my last edition is that the foundation world grew by leaps and bounds in the 1990s, so even if the economy dips, the pool of foundation funders and funds is much larger and deeper than it was in the past. Two other major changes: There are many more filmmakers (partly because access to the means of production keeps decreasing in cost), and market outlets for exhibition/distribution have increased (e.g., new technologies, more cable channels, Internet streaming) and will continue to do so.

Now for a constant that is not about to ever change: Finding funding for noncommercial film and video programs in the U.S. will always be a difficult proposition – for beginning and seasoned filmmakers. That is why this book is here to help. Independently produced film and video programs fulfill a crucial niche in my own personal mission statement as an arts consultant: "To help heal the world through nourishing the arts." I am happy to take a little heat for sounding grandiose; once a professional finds the correct mission statement it's best to live with it no matter the consequences. The media programs created by non-commercial producers of every ilk – documentarians, animators, narrative feature filmmakers, video artists – strike a particular chord in the world that is qualitatively different than commercial product, and that is absolutely necessary for the well being of our society.

If you are a novice filmmaker, this book will give you all the building blocks you need to find support and reduce the number of mistakes beginners always make. If you are a mid-career filmmaker, this book will confirm some things you've always known you should undertake but were tentative about doing, and will teach you some new tricks. If you are a seasoned and established warhorse in the field, then this book will help jumpstart your efforts and re-energize your fundraising plans. If you are not a filmmaker at all, this book will give you both a real-world education on how fundraising for film differs from other forms of fundraising, as well as providing many practical tidbits of fundraising suggestions that are appropriate for any other field (photography, dance, theater, social service, education, et al.).

I want to extend a heartfelt "thanks" to the many filmmakers who allowed their stories to be told in this book (you'll find their names throughout the text), and to: my partner, Evy, for many patient hours of support and proofreading assistance; everyone at Michael Wiese Productions (especially Michael Wiese, Ken Lee, B. J. Markel, and Gina Mansfield); Patrick Murdock, for a wonderful book cover; Thomas Phelps at the NEH; and filmmaker Paul Stekler.

With best wishes for a safe and successful journey ahead,
Morrie Warshawski
www.warshawski.com

LAYING THE FOUNDATION: YOUR CAREER

Filmmaking is a funny business. Part art, part business. Neither fish nor fowl. How does a professional fashion a career in this hybrid environment where the formal training is primarily concerned with art and technique, but rarely with business and career development skills?

Initially, a filmmaker will come to me because of a problem with funding – or rather a problem with a lack of funding. I work almost exclusively with artists in the noncommercial sector who are doing the type of projects that need grants and donations for support. What I have discovered over the years is that funding problems are almost always rooted in a basic set of unresolved career issues. This work has led me to a system of consulting that focuses on helping professionals with career development basics that, in turn, affect every aspect of their work, including fundraising. Below is a quick summary of the main points of my approach to career development work.

First Steps

The first thing I ask every new client to do is to create a **Mission Statement** – a short, succinct encapsulation of their *raison d'etre*. Why are you a filmmaker? What are you trying to accomplish with your work? The filmmaker has to be able to articulate this for herself, and for everyone she meets. This encapsulates the heart of her work. The Mission Statement also helps the filmmaker make day-to-day decisions about what projects to accept or reject, and how to apportion time to be most effective.

The most important aspect of the mission statement is its ability to help the filmmaker articulate and commit to a unique sense of purpose that keeps her centered, and broadcasts to all potential funders and clients that this is a person who is serious about her work and knows what she wants to accomplish. No one wants to work with or fund a filmmaker who is unclear about this central issue.

I had a client once who was very gifted, had done a few excellent award-winning documentaries, but was having no luck fundraising for her next project. As we began our work I asked for her Mission Statement. She said that she didn't have one. We then explored how she was approaching funders. As it happens, she was going to funders and saying, "I'm an accomplished filmmaker. I just want funds to do documentary work, and I'm willing to make a film about anything that is of interest to your foundation." It took a while for me to convince her that her approach was all wrong. She needed to be very clear about why she was making films, and what she hoped to accomplish, otherwise funders would not take her seriously. She took the time to create a Mission Statement that conveyed her true interests, then matched that with a project that she very much wanted to accomplish. After a year of fundraising she was able to raise over $1-million for her next film.

After creating a mission statement, I ask every client to create a **Vision Statement**. The instructions are to pick a point in the future (at least three years out) and to envision as specifically as possible what your life as a filmmaker will be like in that future. I often have my clients draw a picture of this future, and then go back into the picture to identify items/accomplishments that are more important than others.

The Vision is a powerful tool for energizing the movement of a career, and for giving focus to the accomplishments that mean more to a filmmaker than other things. The filmmaker's vision may well change over the years, but it always provides the filmmaker with a set of strong images around which she can create a plan of action.

Two years after giving my "Jumpstarting Your Career" workshop at Seattle's 911 Media Arts Center, I received a call from one of the attendees. I remembered him well because during the workshop he had drawn a particularly vivid and simple set of vision drawings – one showed his present reality as a person sitting by himself in a theater watching a group of people working on a stage, and the second drawing of his future vision showed a theater full of people watching him working on the stage with a crew and actors. "I just called," he said "because I found that drawing I did a couple of years ago and realized that I've gone from being an independent and isolated filmmaker to someone who is working at an agency with lots of creative people, and I'd completely forgotten that this was my dream." Once the vision is located it can have a powerful pull on a filmmaker's next steps.

The last "first step" my clients must accomplish is to identify their set of **Values** – those immutable values that are inherent in all the work they do and infuse all the interactions they have with others. We are stuck with our values, our basic set of beliefs. They follow us wherever we go and dictate how we respond to our significant others, how we act in teams, how we drive our cars or cook our meals. Since we are stuck with these values, the important thing for a filmmaker to do is to recognize these values, bring them to the surface, and broadcast them proudly. In this manner, values serve as a strong attractor and a strong detractor as a filmmaker moves through the professional world picking the projects and people with whom she wants to work.

Next Steps
Once the filmmaker settles all the issues of Mission, Vision, and Values, she can move on to designing a healthy path toward career development. At this point, it helps tremendously if the filmmaker can identify just a few **Major Goals** – both short-term (six to twelve months into the future) and long-term. These goals, on the short-term side, must be reasonable and achievable goals. And, whenever possible, they should be goals that can be quantified (e.g., "finish one short film per year for the next three years" or "learn how to do digital editing using xyz software on my home computer within the next five months").

The goals should be in alignment with the vision the filmmaker created for the future. All the goals should be directed at helping the film-maker make a significant difference in her career.

One exercise I often give is to have the filmmaker create two lists of actions: "Five Quick Wins" and "Five Bold Moves." The quick wins help to define actions that can take place in the short term that will give the filmmaker some quick successes, which are very important for morale. The bold moves help the filmmaker identify larger and riski-er actions that, if taken, can make a major difference to a career. The bold moves are harder to make, and therefore entail a different level of commitment — one that brings the filmmaker to the very center of how serious she may or may not be about her professed choice of career and vision for the future.

If goals are in place, and the filmmaker is very grounded in a career direction that she feels very strongly about, then it's time to consider one of the basic facts of life in filmmaking and every other profession — the fact that it is other people who will help make or break a career. It is at this point in planning that I have clients identify their **Circles of Influence**. Begin by considering the various large areas of career path that you will have to affect or interact with in order to succeed. These might include Studios, Producers, Foundations, Public Television Stations, Cable Networks, and the Press. Next, identify spe-cific organizations and their locations. Then, for each organization identify the names of the people you need to influence. Where you do not know the name, list the title and then find out who fills that posi-tion. Now you have a good rich map full of names that you must fold into your *modus operandi* as you begin to pursue your goals. Place these people on your mail lists, make them aware of you, and meet them in person whenever possible.

Last Steps

Actually there are no last steps in career development. It's an ongoing process that you will probably take with you into retirement when you replace professional development goals with those of personal growth. What a filmmaker can do to help ensure success is concentrate on a few basic concepts. One is a constant feedback loop of evaluation. The task here is to take regular stock of how you are doing against the goals you have set for yourself. Have you met your targets on time? If not, then what has held you back and how can you adjust either the goal or your performance level to keep moving forward?

Another important aspect of career development is the acquisition of a number of "tools" for your toolkit. News releases, resumes, press clippings of feature articles and reviews, festival awards, video clips, kudos letters from prominent people, an attractive Web site, a compelling project "pitch" – these are all strategic tools that when used wisely will be a boon to a growing career. Creative professionals have a large arsenal of these tools and use them when appropriate to help pave the path forward.

One of the more difficult art forms to promote is videoart. I have had a client for a number of years who is a videoartist. When we first met he had already created a small but interesting body of work that was only known by a handful of people. We put together a promotional strategy that fit his temperament and included, among other things: identifying all the people and agencies who were important to his career development; a press release list with street and e-mail addresses; a commitment to sending out news releases every three months; a commitment to creating an attractive postcard for every new work; the creation of a Web site. In the ten years we have worked together his career has taken a quantum leap forward. Of course, it helps that his work is of excellent quality to begin with, but the use of the proper public relation tools has made a tremendous difference.

One last item I must mention, but that is often ignored, is that of an emotional support system. It is very easy for filmmakers to be isolated. That's one reason I've come to dislike the word "independent" and to encourage all my clients to learn to become "interdependent." It is difficult to overstate the importance of networking, of finding other like-minded people with whom you can share information, trade services, and swap horror stories. Get connected. Create support systems and build in time to network regularly.

In sum:
- Clarify and commit to your mission

- Create a clear and compelling vision

- Identify and broadcast your values

- Set ambitious but achievable short-and-long-term goals

- Evaluate your progress and adjust your strategies accordingly

- Interact with the key people in the center of your circles of influence

- Develop a strong set of tools for career development

- Network, network, network!

WHERE'S THE MONEY?

That's an easy question to answer. There is a simple map to follow for finding money, and it is made up almost exclusively of the following (placed in order of their ranking for giving to all noncommercial endeavors of every type – not just film and video – nationwide):

- ○ **Individuals**
- ○ **Government (Federal, State, and Local)**
- ○ **Private Foundations**
- ○ **Corporations**
- ○ **Small Businesses**
- ○ **Other Nonprofit Organizations**

The filmmaker must remember that he is swimming in a sea of money – surrounded by many sources of funding. The difficult decision is choosing which of these sources is the most appropriate for each project so that energy is placed in the right direction. The filmmaker needs to:

- • ceate a fundraising plan
- • identify the most appropriate sources for each project, and then
- • make the "ask" in the most effective way possible.

There are no deep, dark secrets to fundraising and no set of arcane or insanely difficult skills to acquire. Mainly, fundraising is just plain hard work. One thing that complicates fundraising is that it takes a slightly different set of tools to work in each avenue of possible support. Approaching individuals is different from approaching private foundations. The fundraising letter you send to a corporation will be very different from the one you send to a small business.

This chapter introduces you to the broad categories of possible support and provides an overview of the terrain. I will highlight the "upside" and "downside" of each avenue, list the main ways to research each area, and quickly highlight the means of approach. Later in this book I will be giving much more detail how to actually conduct your fundraising approaches (e.g., how to write a grant, how to ask an individual for support).

INDIVIDUALS

Upside: Individuals have traditionally represented around 87% of all the donations given to all noncommercial enterprises of all types in the U.S. Individual donors provide the filmmaker with a vast pool of potential support. If a filmmaker needs money quickly, individuals are the fastest source of support. Many individual donations are possible in a short amount of time. Also, this type of fundraising entails establishing a direct connection with the donor, and generally involves very little paperwork.

Downside: This type of fundraising is very labor-intensive. Donations generally trickle in over long periods of time, and arrive in small to medium amounts. Individual donations are usually in the hundreds of dollars (or less), occasionally in the thousands of dollars, and very rarely in the tens-of-thousands of dollars.

How Do I Find Them?

People with money for film and video projects are everywhere — quite often in the most obvious places, the ones filmmakers might take for granted. Here is a laundry list of places and methods for finding individual donors:

- **In your head.** The filmmaker should take a moment to think about everyone he has ever met who likes him and/or might take an interest in his project. Rummage through memories of parties, past jobs, conversations with friends, business luncheons, and attendance at official receptions.

- **In your Rolodex.** The filmmaker should go through every name in his address book, Rolodex, or electronic organizing device and see if these generate any ideas or leads. Look at each and every name and ask: "Is this a person who could be of some help to me? Is this a person whom I should ask for support? Is this a person who might give me leads to other people or organizations?"

- **In your family.** Do not rule out asking close relatives and friends for support – they are often the first donors to a project. Keep in mind that the vast majority of individual donations come from people with annual incomes below $50,000. Filmmakers are often hesitant to ask friends and family, but if they are suitable and if the filmmaker feels they can afford to help, then the task is to find a comfortable way to make an approach.

- **In your local newspaper.** Check out the appropriate sections of local and national newspapers for people who have shown interest in the topic area of the film (for documentaries), including the business pages and society columns. It is surprising how often newspapers list the causes supported by individuals, and even how much they gave.

- **Throw a brainstorming party.** A very effective way to garner names is to throw a brief evening gathering where the filmmaker asks guests to help brainstorm names of people and organizations that might contribute.

- **Cast out/into the Net.** The Internet is an excellent place to get word out about a filmmaker's project to niche groups and begin to find people of similar interests who might lend support. Look for appropriate Newsgroups and Listserves by topic area and post notes there if the Webmaster will allow it. Establish a Web site and have it linked to other sites where people might want to find you.

- **The Social Register** (available for a dozen major cities).

- **Membership and Donors Lists.** Check the back of annual reports and performance programs from *nonprofit* organizations where target donors are likely to have already contributed. This is a rich source of information on potential donors. The lovely thing about these donor lists is that they almost always provide the amount of money each person gave – an important piece of information.

- *Who's Who.* Editions of *Who's Who* are available nationally and for regions, as well as various professions.

How to Approach Individuals:
- **One-on-One (or Two-on-One).** This is a direct, in-person ask and is statistically the single most effective way to get money. The one-on-one ask may also be the most difficult one to arrange. A variant on this is the over-the-phone ask (only good with people you already know).

- **Fundraising Houseparty.** This is *not* to be confused with a fundraising event where you charge admission. A fundraising houseparty is one where a number of people are invited to an evening soiree at someone's home. Everyone invited understands that a presentation will be given that night about your film, and that participants will have a chance to decide about making a contribution. (For a very detailed description of this type of event, refer to my book, *The Fundraising Houseparty: How to Get Charitable Donations from Individuals in a Houseparty Setting*).

- **Direct Mail.** There are two variants for direct mail approaches:

  - The first is a **personal letter** sent by you to just a few people you know personally, or by an avid supporter who will write to his own friends.

- The second is a **mass mail** appeal sent to a list of possible supporters (members of clubs, organizations, magazine subscribers, etc.).

- **The Internet.** Currently this is a fledgling method of fundraising for filmmakers, but sure to burgeon soon. E-mail letter appeals to individuals is one approach, but only if the recipient feels that the mailing is not a mass "spam" appeal. Linking your letter to a Web site that has more details is a good idea. Listserves and Usenet groups are another way to get information out about your project and your need for support. Typically, this works best if the filmmaker has a cause-related program, and the notice is being sent by an organization that is involved in that cause and has a large membership list.

GOVERNMENT AGENCIES

Upside: When a government source awards a grant it is usually a substantial amount, in the thousands of dollars. Government grants are very easy to research, and agencies that reject you must provide you with feedback on your application if requested.

Downside: In the last few years government grants have shrunk considerably and have become even more competitive than in the past. Paperwork can be very extensive (application, reports, and accounting). Some government agencies are very worried about political scrutiny, so controversial topics have a more difficult time finding support here.

How Do I Do the Research?

There are three levels of government support available: National, State, and Local.

Nationally, the major sources include:

- National Endowment for the Arts
- National Endowment for the Humanities

- Corporation for Public Broadcasting
- Public Broadcasting Service
- Miscellaneous Government Agencies (Forestry, IRS)

On the **State** level there are typically:

- State Arts Agencies
- State Humanities Councils
- State Tourism Boards

On the **Local** level there are very few agencies that give support, but you can look for:

- Local City or Regional Arts Council
- Local/Regional Commerce and Growth Associations
- City Tourism Board

Information on Government sources can be found through:

- **Catalog of Federal Domestic Assistance.** Available in most libraries.

- **Directly from the agencies themselves.** All publish their own guidelines and application forms.

- **Foundation Center Libraries.** Located in most metropolitan centers, these libraries are a great font of information (see detailed note in next section).

- **Internet.** Every Federal agency, and many state and local agencies, now maintain their own Web sites replete with information and, often, downloadable application forms

How to Approach Government Agencies
Very simply: Get the guidelines, determine if you and the agency are a good match, request the application form and fill out as appropriate, and contact a program officer before sending in materials to cover any questions you might have.

PRIVATE FOUNDATIONS

Upside: In the 1990s private foundations experienced an explosion in the size of their endowments and in the numbers in their ranks. Foundations with a variety of interests can be found throughout the U.S. Grants are almost always in the thousands of dollars, and foundations are very easy to research.

Downside: It takes a long time to finally see a dollar from a foundation, and often years of work setting the stage for an ask — six to eighteen months is not unusual. Some foundations meet only once or twice a year, so it is important to be very mindful of deadlines. Paperwork is usually extensive (introductory letter, full grant proposal, follow-up reports, and accounting). Competition for foundation support is always very stiff, and increases when the economy is in a slump.

How Do I Do the Research?
* **Foundation Center Libraries.** These are the first and best places to go. The Foundation Center Libraries contain many books that list foundations, their areas of interest, application procedures, and grants they have given in the past, as well as basic books on how to write grants. The Foundation Center maintains cooperating center branches in every major city in the U.S. For the one closest to you call 1 (800) 424-9836 or visit their Web site at *www.fdncenter.org*.

Their five main branches are as follows:

* New York City, 79 Fifth Avenue, (212) 620-4230
* San Francisco, 312 Sutter St., (415) 397-0902
* Washington, D.C., 1001 Connecticut Ave., N.W., (202) 331-1400
* Cleveland, 1422 Euclid, Suite 1356, (216) 861-1933
* Atlanta, Suite 150, Hurt Bldg., 50 Hurt Plaza, (404) 880-0094

- **Local Public Library.** Most public libraries have all the basic texts. Two main texts are *The Foundation Directory* and the *National Data Book of Foundations*.

- **Foundations Themselves.** Once you have targeted a foundation, always request a copy of their latest annual report and guidelines for grant applications.

- **The World Wide Web**. Most foundations now have their own Web sites; you can discover a wealth of information right there. Often they list an e-mail contact for correspondence. Also, see the Bibliography (page 165) for a list of Internet sources for doing research.

- **Fast Forward and Record**. Yes, watch PBS for any programs that are similar to yours (or rent them), then record the end credits that list all the funders! These are probably the same national and local foundations that will have an interest in your project.

- **Professional Journals.** Both in your topic area and in film/video. Watch for other projects and see where their funding is coming from. AIVF's excellent journal, *The Independent*, is a great source for upcoming grant deadlines.

- **Network.** Start going to as many places as you can where other filmmakers and people in your topic interest meet – parties, cafes, conferences, workshops. These gatherings offer great opportunities for up-to-date information on funding patterns.

How to Approach Foundations

After doing all the research possible and discovering everything there is to know about the foundation (and about your project), try to make an in-person meeting or at least a phone call with the appropriate program officer. If at all possible, avoid having to write an initial letter of inquiry before that personal contact – letters of inquiry make it too easy to be rejected. After that, complete whatever paperwork the foundation requests, which usually takes the form of a full written grant proposal.

CORPORATIONS

Upside: Corporations have many doors to walk through including:

- corporate foundation office
- the CEO or CFO office
- advertising and marketing departments
- community relations, public relations
- human resources
- employee designated contributions

This is a good environment for entrepreneurial filmmakers. Contributions can be made rather quickly. Contributions can come in the form of money, goods, and/or services.

Downside: It is very hard to do research on corporate funding (at least for corporations without official foundations). Corporations are much more interested in "strategic investments" than in pure donations, so the filmmaker's project usually has to provide an advertising, public relations, or promotion benefit to the company. It helps tremendously to have a personal connection, or someone who will provide entrée.

How Do I Do the Research?

- **Foundation Records**. If a corporation has its own foundation, then you can follow the instructions for private foundations above.

- **Newspapers**. The other best source for information is the business section of your local newspaper (and national publications like *The Wall Street Journal*). The newspaper provides great leads on the current fiscal condition of companies. Do not approach a corporation, for instance, at the end of a very bad earnings quarter.

- *The Directory of International Corporate Giving in America.* Available in most libraries.

- **Standard and Poor's** - *Register of Corporations, Directors and Executives.*

- **Magazines:** *Fortune* (see their annual "Fortune 500 List" issue, also available on their Web site), *Advertising Age, Forbes, INC, Fast Company.*

- **Internet**. Find the corporation's Web site and see if there is any information about applying for donations.

- **Annual Reports.** A good way to find out what the corporation is interested in, its fiscal viability, and whether or not it has a department concerned with community affairs.

How to Approach Corporations

For corporate foundations, use the same instructions as for private foundations. In all other instances, you will need to identify the right person in the right office first (e.g., CEO, Director of Marketing, Employee Contributions Representative). Be prepared to tell the corporation exactly how it will benefit from being associated with your project (this usually translates as a strong correlation between your audience and the demographics and/or psychographics of their customers). Provide whatever written materials they might request (sometimes a short letter with a budget, sometimes a full-blown detailed proposal).

SMALL BUSINESSES

Upside: They are everywhere and are very easy to approach. Little or no paperwork is involved, and there are rarely any reporting requirements. Contribution decision is made very quickly – in a matter of days or weeks. Little or no research is necessary.

Downside: Small businesses rarely give money. They are much more likely to provide donated goods and services (free pizzas for the crew, free use of cell phones, free photocopying). Donations are usually modest. Giving is often based on a strong community connection to the project.

How Do I Do the Research?

- **Chamber of Commerce**. Check for their list of members.
- **Business Journal**. Subscribe to or locate your City's edition.
- **Clubs and Associations**. Attend meetings of the local Rotary and Kiwanis Clubs.
- **Local Television**. Watch late night TV to see who advertises.
- **The Better Business Bureau**. A good place to check references.
- **Snoop.** Walk around your neighborhood. Make notes about local businesses and visit them to introduce yourself.
- *The Yellow Pages.* Let your fingers do the walking.

How to Approach Small Businesses

The personal approach works best. Contact the business owner by phone or in person and be prepared to hand over a short document with:

- A very brief description of the project with information on your crew.

- The benefit to the donor. This could be in the form of free publicity through a credit in the film and/or on its packaging, free copies of the videotape, or an invitation to a local premiere where the business will be thanked in public.

- The types of goods/services you are requesting (e.g., three free lunches for a crew of ten, twenty copies of a sixty page script).

- Local references.

OTHER NONPROFITS

Upside: There are some niche pots of money available from organizations and agencies in increasing numbers. Often these are very localized and emphasize a larger number of small grants.

Downside: No long tradition of funding, so research can be difficult, especially as new sources crop up.

How Do I Do the Research?

Ear-to-the-ground, plus all other methods recommended above. In this arena, professional journals are a key source of information. Some agencies that fit in this category include:

- **Religious Denominations**
- **The United Way**
- **Independent Television Service-ITVS** (an agency under the wing of the Corporation for Public Broadcasting)
- **Film Arts Foundation-FAF** (with a re-granting endowment for projects in the San Francisco Bay Area only)
- **Foreign Television Stations** (e.g., Channel Four in Britain, Canal+ in France, ZDF in Germany) who are interested in co-productions
- **Foreign Governments** with grants for co-productions that take place primarily on their soil and/or with local talent
- **Fraternities and Sororities**
- **VFW, Knights of Columbus, Lions Club, Rotary International**

How to Approach Other Nonprofits

The approach will vary in this arena from donor to donor, so there are no pat rules. Foreign entities, for instance, almost always will need to be contacted in person, which makes this type of funding very difficult. ITVS and FAF have printed guidelines available by request. ITVS, especially, has become a key source of funding for independent projects of an alternative nature intended for television. Churches and other nonprofits will need to be researched and approached on a case-by-case basis. Nonprofit service organizations might make an outright donation, or want to make pre-buys of your program as benefits to their members and/or for fundraising purposes.

Mixing it Up

Once the filmmaker has a grasp of the full universe of potential support, the next question is "What mix of fundraising support is the best for me and my project?" A fundraising plan has to be created because no one has the time and the energy necessary to pursue all avenues of possible support. There are some quick guidelines that can help the filmmaker with this issue. The first is to realize that some projects are just more naturally appropriate for some types of support. The second filter is to realize that some filmmakers are more naturally predisposed and skillful at certain types of approaches – these filmmakers are great schmoozers, or wonderful grant writers, or great at working with community members.

With regard to the right "fit" for your project with funders, here is a loose overview:

- **Documentaries.** Social issue documentaries enjoy the broadest possible avenues of support – appropriate for almost every type of fundraising.

- **Independent Dramatic Features and Shorts.** Best bets are individuals approached one-on-one or in fundraising houseparty settings. Occasionally noncommercial features can find grant support from foundations and government agencies, but usually only if there is a social issue involved. Corporate support might be forthcoming if there is product or audience crossover within the interests of the business.

- **Experimental or "Personal" Work.** Video art and experimental films have very limited avenues of support – just a handful of private foundations and a few government agencies. These works rarely receive support from corporations or small businesses. Individuals can be a good source of support, but there usually has to be an already established connection between the filmmaker and the donor.

- **Animated Films.** Very few funders are interested in animation as an art form. If the animated film has any type of "message" or can be used in an educational setting, then funding can be found through all appropriate channels. If the animated work is primarily entertaining and/or personal or experimental in nature, then the filmmaker can look to a few government and private foundations, and perhaps individuals.

In Chapter 4 I will be discussing in more detail the specifics of making each approach more effective. This will help the filmmaker decide which approaches are more suited to her skills, her project, and her resources (time, money, and volunteer support). For instance, the documentary filmmaker might end up deciding that for her one-hour program she will try to pursue the following mix of support:

- 50% from three or four private foundations
- 20% from state humanities councils
- 15% from four fundraising houseparties
- 15% from individuals through a letter writing campaign

Whatever mix chosen, try to pick one that has a high probability of success for you and the project. Sooner or later the filmmaker will have to present this fundraising "plan" to potential donors who will want to feel that it is plausible. More important, sooner or later the filmmaker will actually have to traverse this road toward a goal of adequately funding a project.

PATCHWORK QUILT – PUTTING YOUR PROJECT TOGETHER

Filmmakers who come to me for advice have usually "hit the wall" in fundraising efforts – they have tried everything possible to acquire support for a project but just can't seem to get past a certain point. I am often placed in the position of having to figure out and tell film-makers what they are doing wrong so we can understand why their rate of rejection is so high. I said earlier that many fundraising problems are rooted in basic career development issues (e.g., comportment, mission, professional direction). There is one other great impediment to funding: hitting the street before the filmmaker is actually ready to fully articulate the project in a logically convincing and emotionally engaging manner.

The Story That Had to Be Told

What the filmmaker must ask before beginning to fundraise is: "Do I know everything I must know about this project before I approach a funder? Can I answer any potential questions about my project that anyone might ask me?" Too many filmmakers start looking for money before they have done the very basic groundwork on their project, and this lack of preparation leads to a number of quick rejections by potential funders. When I ask filmmakers how they got involved with projects, they often say, "I ran across this incredible story/per-son/organization and I knew immediately that this was a story that must be told." I have heard this sentence almost word-for-word so often that it must be a virus specific to independent filmmakers.

What I have never heard a filmmaker say is, "This is a story that must be heard." In other words, the filmmaker must realize that even though the idea for the film fills her with great excitement and she feels an overwhelming compulsion to tell it, she still must prove that a lot of other people will feel the same way and want to hear her story. She will have to fully address basic questions of need, audience, distribution, marketing, crew and staff, and budget. Until these are all as well articulated as possible, it is a mistake to start looking for financial support.

Question Number One is always "need." Is there a need in the world for one more film about XYZ? I ask my clients the following questions: "Can you name the first five titles of other films that people will think of immediately when you mention your new film?" If the filmmaker says "no" then I know more homework needs to be done.

Every film fits into some niche where it will be clustered with other similar titles or subjects. The filmmaker has to do the research that uncovers all other similar films, and where any of these films seem very close in content, the filmmaker must make an effort to actually see those films. No funder wants to place support behind a program that has already been made by another filmmaker. There are many ways to uncover the titles of your "competition": filmographies and videographies available in libraries, catalogs from distributors of films in your genre or subject area, conversations with experts in the field, lists of programs aired on PBS, and the Internet Movie Database (*www.imdb.com*).

Keep in mind that when you make your initial pitch to funders, whether or not they articulate it out loud, they will be thinking "I know another film or two that's about the exact same subject – how is this any different?" The filmmaker must be ready to **differentiate** her project from all others that have already been created. She has to be ready to say, "My program is different from all others in the following ways..."

Here are some areas where a filmmaker can make a case for significant differentiation from another similar project:

- **Timing:** The project is much more current than anything previously created, and contains brand new information.

- **Depth:** The project is longer and goes into much more depth on the subject than any other previous film.

- **Content:** The project covers issues and aspects of the topic that have never been covered before and/or from a different perspective.

- **Style:** The project will be the first animated/narrative/verité documentary on the subject ever made.

- **Audience:** The project will be made for a particular audience (the elderly, young children, illegal immigrants) who has never had access to this information.

The idea is a very simple and basic one: Make sure the project is significantly different from anything else currently available. Be able to convince people that there is a genuine need in the world for this film because it has something important to say in a way that hasn't been heard before. When I cover the elements of the perfectly written proposal, I will be advising the inclusion of a whole section on this topic in the grant.

One important principle to remember when differentiating your project from others is to *never say anything negative about other films and/or filmmakers*. It is a mistake to differentiate the program by saying "My film will be better than the others because they are all substandard works of filmmaking, and mine will be a beautiful and professional work of art." Even if this is true, saying this only places the filmmaker in an unflattering light.

Audience

Sooner or later the filmmaker wants the work to reach an audience. Deciding who that audience will be is something that should happen as early in the project as possible. If I ask a filmmaker who her audience is, I usually get the following answer: "Everybody!" Unfortunately, not only is this answer inaccurate and implausible (no film ever made could possibly appeal to everyone), this answer will not please funders, and it keeps the filmmaker from creating a program that is likely to really appeal to specific segments of the population.

Whom does the filmmaker want to reach? What types of people are most likely to be interested in the project? Among whom does the filmmaker want to make an impact?

Start by trying to draw circles of broad audience types, including but not limited to:

- Geography
- Age
- Race
- Gender
- Sex
- Sexual Orientation
- Religion
- Lifestyles, Hobbies, Leisure Interests
- Occupation
- Income Level
- Educational Background
- Political Affiliation

The filmmaker can begin to define the particular demographics and psychographics that make up the audience to be reached. For instance, a documentary might be geared to upper-middle-class women over thirty who live in urban environments throughout the U.S. and who are at a high risk for breast cancer, or the film might be targeted to young black males between the ages of thirteen and eighteen who come from single parent households.

There are important lessons to be learned from this exercise. The first is that the program's content and format might need adjusting so that it is better suited to the correct audience. Another lesson might be that the intended audience is too poor to afford the program, so funds for distribution will have to be added to the fundraising budget. The filmmaker should consider if this list has already begun to lead to ideas for finding support (e.g., prominent individuals and affinity organizations).

For the filmmaker who sincerely believes her film is being made for everybody, I suggest a process of elimination — *a reductio ad absurdum*. Start making lists of just the narrowest audience types imaginable who would in no way be interested in the film: Bedouin nomads, children under six, people who belong to religions that forbid watching television or movies. Eventually this process will help the filmmaker to back in to the audience.

Occasionally a filmmaker might embark on a project and actually not know who the potential audience is; the filmmaker only knows that the topic is compelling and that somebody out there must want to see it. In that case, I advise creating a process to start *finding* the audience as early as possible — ideally well before the project reaches completion. This can be done in any number of creative ways, including:

- Holding works-in-progress screenings with different focus groups
- Circulating the treatment or script to people the filmmaker trusts
- Consulting with experts in the subject area of the film
- Talking to distributors and exhibitors

It will be very difficult to get funding support from sophisticated funders until the filmmaker can articulate just whom she hopes to reach.

When Bruce Sinofsky and Joe Berlinger set out to make their documentary, *Brother's Keeper*, they were convinced they had a compelling story that everyone would want to see – even though they had shot in black and white and the subjects of the film were three elderly dairy farmers, accused of murder, who might have been involved in incest. The filmmakers received the cold shoulder treatment from distributors who could not figure out the identifiable target group, and the filmmakers themselves could not articulate the audience. Sinofsky and Berlinger spent the next year of their lives in self-distribution – an effort that might have been spared had they gotten a better sense of their audience early in the process.

Distribution

Once the question of need is answered, and the target audiences have been identified, the next piece of the puzzle is distribution – how the filmmaker intends to get the completed program out to the world. Distribution has become a central concern for funders. They are well aware of one of the sad facts of life in independent filmmaking: Many films are made, but few are seen by their full intended audience.

This is why it is smart to talk to bona fide distributors very early in the process of your thinking about and creating a project. Distributors are a great font of practical, real-world information on the potential for marketing a program and making sure it reaches viewers. Begin the process of identifying the perfect distributors of the film being made. There are lists of distributors of independent film and video programs that can be found on the Internet. A number of books list distributors (a good one is the *AIVF GUIDE TO FILM AND VIDEO DISTRIBUTORS*). Catalogs are often available in libraries and in institutions that purchase media products. Other filmmakers are also a great source of advice about distributors.

I recommend doing some homework on the distributors that are appropriate, and then picking up a phone and calling them directly for a conversation (perhaps preceded by an introductory e-mail). What questions can be asked of a distributor at this early state in a project?

- Is there really a need for the project in the marketplace?
- Is the project the right length and format for the audience?
- What is the potential for sales in dollars and units over what length of time?
- Are other similar projects in the pipeline?
- Does this program have to have a study guide and/or a Web site?

If the distributor is enthusiastic about the project, be sure to ask for a letter of support — this is the most credible evidence that can be given to a funder to help prove the eventual viability of a program. Get these letters whenever possible.

I had a client once who was creating a three-hour series on the environment for grade school children. He called a distributor who was very excited by the idea because it had not been done before, and teachers were making requests for anything he might have on the topic. The filmmaker was ecstatic, until the distributor told him the following: "I love your idea, but I can't take your series." The filmmaker wanted to know why. The distributor answered, "Because you're making three one-hour films. In my market, teachers want either twenty-minute or thirty-minute films." Now the filmmaker knew that if he could cut his work to have natural twenty or thirty-minute sections he would have a much better chance at reaching his audience. Imagine how expensive this lesson would have been had he waited until after completing his three-hour series to talk to a distributor.

The filmmaker will have to resolve the entire landscape of the eventual distribution of the program. What markets will the program explore and in what sequence? Broadly, the markets include:

- **Festivals**
- **Theatrical**
- **Cable Television** (Pay Per View, Premium Channels, Basic Cable, Public Access)
- **Public Television** (national and local)
- **Commercial Broadcast Television**
- **Home Video**
- **Educational Markets**
- **Organizations, Associations, and Libraries**
- **Catalogs**
- **The Internet**
- **Domestic and International outlets** for all of the above

Do not make the mistake of telling a funder that the sole intended distribution outlet is PBS. Funders want to see a distribution plan that is much more rich and varied than just Public Television. Increasingly, funders are also interested in knowing about specific marketing/public relations plans, community outreach plans, and whether or not a Web site will be created in conjunction with the film.

I like to ask funders about their pet peeves. One funder confided the following to me: "If a filmmaker tells me that her only method of distribution will be a PBS broadcast, then I won't fund her. I need to hear a distribution plan that is much more varied and multifarious than just PBS, otherwise I can't make the grant."

Good Company
The crew that works on the film can be a defining factor in whether or not a funder feels comfortable investing their funds in a project. The first thing to decide is what role the filmmaker will play in the project – writer, director, producer, cinematographer, editor. Next, the filmmaker must decide who will make up the rest of the team. There are

very few formulas for fundraising success that I will give in this book. Almost all fundraising is a vast gray area, with very little black-and-white clarity because so many things depend on the specific project and the filmmaker. However, there is one rule that applies to all projects looking for donations:

> *The less experienced the filmmaker, the more experienced the crew must be. The more experienced the filmmaker, the less experienced the crew needs to be.*

The issue here is very simply one of credibility. Generally, funders are more comfortable dealing with filmmakers who have a proven track record. Emerging filmmakers doing their first or second program, and who have not raised large amounts of money before or earned any critical accolades or awards, are at a distinct disadvantage. They are still climbing that steep hill of credibility. In those instances, I tell the filmmaker to attach experienced people to their projects in key roles. I also highly recommend finding someone with an excellent reputation to act as an advisor to the project. Get that person to write a letter that says he agrees to make available a certain number of hours or days at a certain rate of pay, during which he will provide assistance to the project. I have seen many young filmmakers have success fundraising because they were able to attach well-known artists to their projects.

I explained this tactic once to an emerging filmmaker who had an ambitious project on the drawing board. I asked what filmmakers she respected most. One name popped up immediately: a filmmaker with a long history of creating excellent ethnographic documentaries. As it happens, I knew that this filmmaker lived in her city and was listed in the phonebook, so I encouraged her to give him a call. She was frightened about the prospect of a "cold call" so we did a quick role-play. Then she made the call and, miraculously, the filmmaker answered the phone himself. They had a great conversation, he invited her to have lunch with him, and soon he had signed a letter of agreement to serve as an official advisor to the project. The filmmaker wrote his day rate into her budget, attached his letter of commitment to all her grant proposals, and it made a significant difference in boosting her credibility and acquiring funds for her project.

Good Timing

Funders are also going to want to know how long it will take to complete the program. Unfortunately, a true answer is usually, "Longer than I promised!" Films almost always take longer to complete than is initially predicted. The main reason for this is that fundraising is unpredictable and never comes together as quickly or as easily as we would like. The filmmaker needs to step back and begin to think about the long-term implication of embarking on a noncommercial film project. If everything goes as planned, the entire process – from thinking of the idea, through fundraising, production, postproduction, and entering distribution – might take as little as three years. Most of my clients would consider this a speedy schedule. However, ambitious projects that entail large sums of money might take much longer. Even small projects about difficult subject matter can take much longer. It is not at all unusual for a project to eat up five or more years of a filmmaker's life.

What must be presented to funders is a time line for the entire project that shows a good-faith estimate for how long all the various parts of the project would take from conception all the way through the beginning of distribution, if there were no unusual interruptions. It is much smarter to overestimate the time than to underestimate. I often tell clients it is going to take 50% more time to do the project than they predict.

A typical time line should be generic in terms of years/months and not chronologically specific. In other words, never say "I will begin research on June 1st, and go into production on August 28th, then edit the program in December." What invariably happens is that as the project progresses all these dates get changed. It is much better to show all elements in blocks of time. Here is a sample of a simple generic time line.

Activity	Year One				Year Two				Year Three			
Quarter	1st	2nd	3rd	4th	1st	2nd	3rd	4th	1st	2nd	3rd	4th
Research	x											
Fundraising	x	x	x	x	x	x	x	x	x			
Script Writing			x									
Preproduction				x	x							
Production						x	x					
Postproduction								x	x	x		
Distribution											x	

With this time line in hand, the filmmaker can say to the funder, "This is how long each aspect of my project will take, and how long the entire effort will go, if there are no interruptions and if fundraising moves smoothly."

Money Matters

Budgeting, like distribution, is a science in and of itself. There are whole books written on these topics and I recommend reading them if these areas are new to a filmmaker. What I have found with budgets is that they are accurate mirrors of most things that are either right or wrong with a project. I often read a project budget before I look at the narrative description. When I read a budget I am looking for a story. Too often I find myself reading a mystery, a comedy, or a horror story, when what I am looking for is a good romance.

After determining all the other elements of a project it is time to sit down and create a fiscal representation of what it will take to make the filmmaker's dream a reality. This exercise must be done on a computer using some type of spreadsheet program, and not on a calculator, or by using a pencil and accounting paper. Why? Because in filmmaking as in life, *things change*. This may be truer in filmmaking than in most other art forms because of the length of time involved to create new work. In any event, the only environment for budget forecasting that is amenable to change is the computer spreadsheet, where you can change one or two figures in a very complicated budget and have everything else change instantaneously.

To begin a project, consider creating two different budgets. Budget Number One is the **Best Case Scenario Budget**. For this budget figure out reasonable cash costs for everything you need to create the project in just the way that would make it a perfect program that meets a certain set of standards. This will be the budget that is used to begin fundraising and will be shown to potential funders in one form or another throughout the process.

Budget Number Two is the **Worst Case Scenario Budget**. This budget is more important than the first, but it will never be shown to anyone. It is the budget that is kept in a drawer and only pulled out when the filmmaker "hits the wall" and is finally fed up with fundraising and just wants to finish up as soon as possible. For this budget, go through every item in the detailed Best Case Scenario asking "How can I eliminate, reduce, beg, borrow, or steal items to make this budget as small as possible *but still create a program of which I am proud?"* A filmmaker should never cross over a line of minimum standard and self-respect. But, generally there is quite a bit of wiggle room between the ideal budget and one that is more livable. After the minimum amount has been reached in fundraising, the filmmaker will have to assess whether or not the effort needed to raise more funds is worth the value added to the program.

The entire budget can be built around a simple grid showing for each budget item: Number, Frequency, Cost Basis, Total. Later, as things get more complicated, "Total" will be divided into two separate columns showing "Cash" and "In-kind." An in-kind contribution is one where someone is providing either a service or some goods as a donation and not asking for a cash payment. For instance, a lab might provide $10,000 worth of services at a 30% discount — so the budget would show $7,000 cash, $3,000 in-kind and a total of $10,000. Still later, when the project is off and rolling, the filmmaker is going to add yet another subdivision that shows "Amount Raised To-Date" and "Cash Still Needed."

Get in the habit of adding notes to any and all budget items that might eventually draw a question from a funder. Be liberal with these notes as they will help with funders who are inexperienced reading film budgets. Most funders will accept an unusually high cost for an item if there is a good reason for it. For instance, I worked once with filmmakers who showed a twenty-to-one shooting ratio which was going to entail very high film stock costs and extra processing expenses. Their reasoning was that they would be shooting in a part of the world where they would not have access to film stock if they ran out, and where they had only one chance to shoot and get it right. They wrote this explanation as a note directly on their budget and funders had no problem accepting the expense as being valid.

In general, here are some basic tips and notes for noncommercial film project budgets:

- **Fair and Comparable.** The simple rule of thumb for deciding what to pay for any item on the budget is whatever is *fair and comparable for the experience of the person doing the work, the* *type of work being done, and the city where the work takes place.* For many types of work and for many types of purchases, fair and comparable will vary widely from one location to another.

- **Pay Yourself!** Funders are suspicious of budgets that show the filmmaker paying herself nothing. It makes the filmmaker very suspect in the eyes of the funder. Filmmakers must begin budgets assuming that some fair level of payment will be coming to them, even if they know in their bones that they are ready to donate time when needed if it will help complete the project.

- **Red Flags.** Go through the budget line-by-line and identify every item that might raise a red flag, then write an explanatory note.

- **Contingency.** A contingency is a percentage that is often added to film costs in case the film goes over budget. It is a safety net that almost every film needs, and is common in commercial budgets. However, in the nonprofit world, only include contingencies at the end of a budget when the funder has specifically said they would allow a contingency, or when the funder is very familiar with supporting film projects. Otherwise, it is best to not include any contingency at all. Funders unfamiliar with filmmaking will look at the contingency and immediately dismiss it, saying to themselves "If I give the filmmaker money for a contingency she will definitely spend it, and if I don't she can probably finish the film for the lesser amount." So, my best advice is decide on a contingency percentage that feels fair and comfortable for the project, and then go ahead and factor it in to each item as you do the budget.

- **In-Kind Donations.** Most funders do not like to support projects that show a very high percentage of in-kind donation as part of the total budget. There are a couple of situations where in-kind donations are helpful. The first is early in the fundraising for a project, at its beginning stages when not much cash has yet been donated. Having commitments for in-kind donations from businesses and individuals shows that the project has some support and is being taken seriously. Another type of project where a high level of in-kind support is acceptable is a modestly budgeted project that is community-based, where free labor and the donation of goods can make a tremendous difference.

• **Equipment Purchase.** Rarely will a foundation allow its funds to be used for the purchase of equipment. I would avoid ever including the purchase of equipment in a budget, even if the lease/rental amount exceeds the price of purchase. By the way, if the filmmaker happens to already own a piece of equipment being used in a production, then it is fair to include a comparable rate of rental in the budget.

• **Distribution.** At the end of the budget, be sure to include funds to begin a distribution effort. Some costs that can be listed are: Production Stills, Press Packets, Videocassette Screeners, Graphic Design Fee, Festival Entry Fees. If the film is going to the non-theatrical educational market, then funds for a teacher's guide should be added.

Nonprofit — A Definition

In this book I deal only with how filmmakers can convince donors to give money to projects that are inherently noncommercial in nature. The filmmaker needs to make a very basic decision upon embarking on a project. Is the film primarily a noncommercial effort that might accidentally have a commercial life, or is it a project from which the filmmaker fully hopes and intends to make a profit? There are no laws that limit a project that begins in the nonprofit world from going ahead to make a profit once it enters distribution. And there are no laws that preclude a project from receiving money from donors, and investment dollars from investors.

I once acted as Executive Producer on a feature starring the then little-known Danny Glover. When we ran out of our funds from the Rockefeller Foundation, the director turned to a friend of his for finishing funds in the form of an investment, which was repaid when we sold the home video rights. Some other grant-supported independent films that have gone on to make a profit include Spike Lee's first feature, *She's Gotta Have It*, and *Hoop Dreams*.

If the film in question is truly being made for educational purposes where the intent is more one of good conscience than profit, then the project is probably best off staying in the world of nonprofit donations and grants. If the project is clearly being made in order to recoup investment and create a profit, then it is better off staying in the commercial arena and looking for loans and/or investments. Filmmakers seeking investments will need to prepare a Private Placement Memorandum and comply with securities law – issues not covered in this book.

I recommend a simple test for deciding if a project that has a non-commercial intent should truly stay in that world or perhaps cross over into the world of commercial financing. I bring this up because if this route – investments – is open to the film, it is a much easier road to follow than the path of looking for grants and donations. My test entails doing the following:

- Calculate the total expense of producing the film and placing it into distribution.

- Next, create three income scenarios from all the possible distribution markets that you enumerated earlier – best case, middle case, and worst case.

- Go to your worst case income total and deduct from it your total expenses.

If the calculation shows a profit, or comes up close to being even, then save yourself a whole lot of time and trouble by forgetting about donations. Take out a loan, use a credit card, or find a few investors.

Your Umbrella - The Fiscal Sponsor

Let me be clear about the distinction between a donor and an investor. A donor is someone (or some agency) that is willing to donate money, goods, or services to a project without expecting any money back in return. An investor is someone who, when placing money, goods, or services into a project, is promised a return on that "investment" under certain conditions. The investor wants a piece of the action, and the donor wants only a receipt for a tax-deductible charitable donation plus the knowledge that something important will be created to help make the world a better place. This is a bit of a simplification, but the basic outline holds true.

The important wrinkle for an independent filmmaker is that in order for a donor to receive credit for a tax-deductible charitable donation, that donation must be given to a bona fide nonprofit organization — known by the IRS classification as a 501(c)(3). The filmmaker therefore has two choices:

1. Create her very own 501(c)(3) organization.

2. Find a Fiscal Sponsor — another nonprofit organization that already has 501(c)(3) status.

Opinions are split on which of these two routes is best. Generally, if the filmmaker has plans of making many noncommercial programs with substantial budgets over many years, then creating a nonprofit entity makes sense. The downside to this route is that it takes time to file the paperwork and receive nonprofit status from the IRS (eight months to a year is normal), and once the entity is created the filmmaker will need to file annual papers plus create a Board of Trustees who have ultimate legal control. There are a number of books that provide great advice on this process. The assistance of a lawyer will be necessary and this can be quite expensive unless the legal assistance is partially or totally *pro bono*. Sometimes a local chapter of the national organization called Volunteer Lawyers for the Arts can be of some initial help.

Otherwise, it is very easy for a filmmaker to find a Fiscal Sponsor to serve as the umbrella for the project. Who can be a fiscal sponsor? Any organization that already has nonprofit status. These include media arts centers, hospitals, schools, associations. Some well-known fiscal sponsors for filmmakers include the Film Arts Foundation (San Francisco), the New York Foundation for the Arts, Women Make Movies (New York), the International Documentary Association (Los Angeles), 911 Media Arts (Seattle), and many others.

At the most simple level, the sponsor will accept checks for your project (e.g., the donor writes the check made out to the fiscal sponsor with your project as the beneficiary in the "note" or "for" section at the bottom of the check). Then the fiscal sponsor deposits that check and returns most or all of that money to the filmmaker. Fiscal Sponsors and filmmakers negotiate what percentage will be kept by the umbrella organization for this service. An average range is currently between 5% and 10% – although I have seen some filmmakers negotiate a 0% fee, and I have also seen charges as high as 60%! A fiscal sponsor can do much more than just be a conduit for funds. The sponsor might also provide accounting services, advice about fundraising, connections with donors, and give office space and use of equipment.

Follow some basic common sense guidelines when setting up an arrangement with a fiscal sponsor:

- Pick a fiscal sponsor who is trustworthy and who sincerely appreciates the worth of the film being made.

- Demand that there is a written legal agreement.

- Make it clear that the filmmaker is the sole owner of copyright (e.g., this is not a "work for hire").

- Make it clear that the fiscal sponsor has no creative control of the project.

- Enumerate exactly how funds will be deposited, what happens to any earned interest, and under what schedule the film-maker will receive payments once donations are made.

Once the agreement is sealed, have the sponsor write a very strong letter of support addressed "To Whom It May Concern," in which the sponsor gives the reasons for wanting to help with this project, and urges other to help provide support. Also, get a copy of the sponsor's official letter from the IRS giving it nonprofit status. Both documents will be needed as fundraising progresses.

One last note about fiscal sponsors: A project can have more than one fiscal sponsor. This is important for projects that take place in more than one state and might need local sponsors to get donations from foundations or agencies that cannot donate out of their state. It is not unusual to receive donations from a couple of state humanities councils, for instance, that might have to write checks to entities within their state boundaries. Just make sure your agreements with fiscal sponsors are non-exclusive and that everyone knows who is on board.

Now we can finally hit the streets and start looking for money!

GETTING PERSONAL - INDIVIDUAL DONORS

In Chapter 2, "Where's the Money," I outlined the basic methods for identifying individuals who might contribute to a project, and the approaches that are appropriate for this type of fundraising. This chapter will take a closer and more detailed look at the nuts-and-bolts of this particular fundraising path.

If it is true that the vast majority of all the donations that go to all nonprofit endeavors in the U.S. come from individuals, why is it that more filmmakers do not pursue this path? I would suggest there are reasons external to the filmmaker, and there are internal barriers as well. One external reason might be that individual donors tend not to provide large donations. And, by "large" I mean in the tens of thousands of dollars. For a project that is looking for hundreds of thousands of dollars in support, it might be physically difficult to garner enough donations from individuals to raise the full budget.

However, even when medium and modest amounts of support could make a tremendous difference to a project, filmmakers often do not pursue this route of fundraising. The internal barriers are usually a fear of asking and a discomfort with being in a position of having to personally make an ask. It is so much easier to write a grant proposal than to sit across a table from someone, look them in the eye, and ask for support.

Fact is, there is no more effective way to get a donation than to make a person-to-person request; and, if money is needed quickly, there is no faster way to get support. Close this book right now, go make a phone call to a relative, and there might be a check in the mail tomorrow! If a filmmaker wants to get very good at fundraising, the internal impediments to making an ask must be addressed. Often the fear of rejection or the discomfort with requesting support can be overcome by remembering why the project is being made in the first place, and the importance it has for its potential audience. The film-maker must feel, deep down, that the world will be a much better place once the film is completed.

One other upside to approaching individuals for support is that this type of fundraising has a healthy byproduct – it forces filmmakers to interact with the community, and brings the filmmaker face-to-face with a funder. When the check gets handed over the donation becomes "personal" and the connection between the filmmaker and the funder is so much more real than when a grant is received through the mail. I recommend that the novice fundraiser conduct some role-playing exercises with friends to help practice asking sce-narios and to begin to find some comfort level with dealing directly with donors.

The Pitch
One of the very basic tools needed for all the fundraising venues is the pitch – a very short statement that tells the listener what the film is about, who it is for, and what is interesting or unusual about it. The pitch helps generate a conversation. How long should the pitch be? My recommendation is about twenty seconds! In other words, just long enough to pass the rigors of the infamous "elevator test":

> *If someone got on an elevator with me and asked what I was working on, could I interest them in my project before they reached the next floor?*

If your pitch does not pass this test, it needs more work. Filmmakers often make the mistake of putting together lengthy descriptions of their projects and failing to remain sensitive to the fact that most peo-ple make up their minds about things very quickly. The listener has decided within a matter of seconds whether or not he is bored or intrigued by the filmmaker and the project being pitched. If the listener is bored, then talking for more than a minute is not going to help your cause. If the listener is intrigued, then the very best thing a filmmaker can do is to pause and allow questions so that a dialogue — and not a monologue — can take place.

Early in the project create a short and exciting pitch that can be used in any and all settings. The pitch will get used thousands of times before the project is completed. There is no one perfect formula for creating a pitch because of the tremendous variety of projects and personalities. However, there are some guidelines that can help create a dynamic pitch. The screenwriter and author William Goldman (*Adventures in the Screen Trade*) gives some good advice about pitching:

- Be passionate
- Identify the audience
- Never forget whom you are talking to
- Be brief
- Remember you are not telling a story — you are throwing out a hook
- Keep it simple
- One or two lines
- Grab them
- Pitch ten times a day

In a *New York Times* interview (January 2, 2003) the producer Ismail Merchant (*Howard's End, Remains of the Day*) says the following about his talent for separating people from their money to finance a film: "It is... a matter of 'injecting your enthusiasm about something you are doing, which you feel is so exceptional that it would be a pleasure for someone to be involved in it.'"

A participant in one of my workshops told a story about the power a good pitch can have in almost any type of setting. The filmmaker was standing in line at a grocery store waiting to check out. The line was pretty long, and she ended up having a conversation with the man just behind her. At one point he asked her what she did for a living. She replied, "I'm a filmmaker." "Oh," he replied, "what an interesting profession. What are you working on now?" It was at this point that she used her pitch for a documentary she was doing that took place in Turkey. "My gosh," said the man, "I'm from Turkey! Tell me more about your project." The man asked for her business card before paying for his groceries. Three weeks later the filmmaker received a five-figure donation for her project. Never underestimate the power of a well-crafted pitch, and be ready to pitch *any and everywhere*.

Below are some pitches of actual films. Look through them to find ones that work, and ones that would not hold the interest of a listener. See if these good and bad examples can provide ideas for creating a powerful pitch for your own film.

- Eating disorders affect 57% of women over 40. *Hunger Artists* tells the story of a group of women who ban together to overthrow the diet industry.

- *Radius* is the story of a female pilot who crash lands on a planet behind enemy lines. She has twenty minutes to escape the blast radius of a ticking doomsday bomb activated by the crash.

- American culture has a one-dimensional image of older women. My one hour documentary, *Acting Our Age*, plans to smash these images through personal portraits of six ordinary women in their 60's and 70's who share their lives in candid interviews that tackle a range of thought-provoking topics: self-image, sexuality, financial concerns, dying, and changing family relationships. Along the way we'll meet role models who show a vibrant strength of spirit and inspiring zest for life, and forever change our notions of growing old and female in America.

- *Crossing* defies description – superficially a comedy/thriller, it bends genres as well as genders in the story of a clever but confused young mobster who has problems with a secret fetish and a hooker he falls for on the eve of his wedding.

- *Licensed to Kill*, a riveting journey into the minds of men who have murdered homosexuals, is a kaleidoscopic montage of interviews with killers behind prison bars, actual footage of gay bashings and murders, on-the-spot news stories, and videotaped confessions of the inmates themselves. This film is a chilling investigation into anti-gay violence and the homophobic attitudes that perpetuate hate crimes against gay men and lesbians.

- Play is not trivial – it's fundamental to the development of humans and all other animals. My three-part series, *The Promise of Play*, will look at play among chimpanzees, Mardi Gras celebrants, dot.com companies, police officers, and doctor Patch Adams – all in an effort to show how play allows us to gain greater benefit in our individual, group, and political lives.

- Our film was inspired by real events and is indicative of the kind of work that our company is committed to creating. Briefly, *Tabbatha*, a portrait of a young, unwed mother, follows a day in the life of the title character. Uneducated, unprepared for motherhood, herself the daughter of a single mother, Tabbatha struggles to maintain composure as she encounters the hard facts of her life, a struggle she ultimately loses. Overwhelmed by the isolation of single-motherhood in a suburb and the irrefutable presence of her newborn, she impetuously commits the unthinkable and attempts to conceal her crime, before seeking refuge in the banalities of young suburban life. It is a compelling story, again based on real events. It is story that we believe (and we hope you agree) needs to be told.

- *Must Be Love* is a crackling good romantic comedy about the crazy things men do for love. Set in Cornwall, two best friends become rivals in love when their high school flame returns to their small town. (Think *Waking Ned* meets *Sleepless in Seattle*.) Academy Award nominated for *Fatal Attraction*, Hollywood star Anne Archer and two well-known English actors, Bryan Murray and Joe McGann, are featured. Helen, a middle-aged woman who has found fame and fortune in the fashion world of North America, visits the Cornish town she left behind as a teenager. Her childhood friends, Ian and Gavin – one now a widower, one forever a roamer – are still infatuated with Helen and her reappearance quickly reawakens old rivalries. The movie is aimed squarely at the audience in the 30-54 age group.

Qualify the Donor

Once a list of possible donors has been identified (see my instructions for this in Chapter Two), the next important step is to "qualify" each of the donors – find out as much as possible about each person on the list. The kind of information needed includes:

- **Who the donor likes to support.** Individual donors are similar to private foundations in that they usually have a "theme" to their giving – a type of cause or area of interest where they want to give their support. This might be the arts and culture, animal rights, the environment, or any number of causes. It is very unusual for someone to be open to giving money to any and all types of nonprofit endeavors. Identify what they like.

- **What the donor likes to give.** Typically, individuals have the following types of things they like to donate: Money, Volunteer Time, Professional Goods and Services. Some people like to give money. Others are just more comfortable (either because of their economic standing or their philosophy) giving their time and expertise volunteering for a project. And still others like to give goods (equipment, for instance) or donated services (like catering). Once this information is known, the filmmaker can see if there is a good match for the needs of the project.

- **The donor's comfort level of giving.** Many a donation has been won or lost because of the amount requested. Individuals are funny about how they give money − they have a fairly narrow range of money that they typically give to their list of charities. For some people this might be $25 to $35 per ask. For others the range might be $5,000 to $6,000. This information must be researched and discovered *before* making an ask.

- **The approach that works best with the donor.** Although we know from statistics that the most effective approach to gaining a donation is an in-person meeting, it turns out that some donors are just highly resistant to this approach, or are more likely to give under a different scenario. For some donors, a written letter will be effective. For others, they will need to be asked by a peer, perhaps in a fundraising houseparty setting.

There are many ways to qualify the donor list. The very best way is to ask other people in the community who know the donor. One of the great secrets in donor relations is that there are very few secrets. The giving patterns of most people are fairly transparent and known by many other people. This is one reason I am fond of the fundraising brainstorming party where people help generate names of people and organizations who might give to a film project. Someone in that room is highly likely to be able to qualify the donor.

If it is hard to identify one person with knowledge of the donor's giving patterns, try working backwards. Find out what types of charities the donor likes, and what specific organizations the donor has supported. Check organization annual reports to see what amounts the donor typically gives to each (you will find the amounts are very similar). Contact one or two grantees personally and see if they will be willing to talk to you about the donor and provide some tips to help with the ask.

I met a filmmaker once in Los Angeles who told me how she got her first donation for her first documentary. She had been doing commercial work for corporate executives. When she started her personal project she remembered that one of the CEOs she knew had grown up in the neighborhood she planned to document. Before calling him up, she did a little research. She read the annual reports and program notes from local charities and discovered that he was a major donor to cultural causes, and liked to give $20,000 gifts. When she called, she pitched her project and asked permission to send the CEO a full project proposal. His reply was, "Of course I'd like to read your full proposal. I have a deep emotional connection to that neighborhood and I respect your work as a filmmaker. But first, why don't you just tell me how much you want to ask for." The filmmaker said, without hesitating, "What I could really use is $20,000 to help me do some more research, an initial shoot, and create a good fundraising video-clip." His reply was, "Don't bother to send me your proposal, I'm just going to go ahead and write you a check right now!" If the filmmaker had not "qualified" her donor, when she made the ask she might have made the tragic mistake of asking for $5,000 and then feeling lucky she had gained so much money, when in reality she would have lost $15,000.

Research is a basic task that must take place in every venue of fundraising. Researching individual donors – their needs, desires, and giving patterns – is just as important as the type of research on private foundations and government agencies that we will discuss later in this book. Now let's look at the various types of approaches.

One-on-One
For many filmmakers – both novice and experienced – this is the most difficult type of ask to make. Even so, the in-person, face-to-face ask is the hardest one for a donor to resist. Try to make this type of ask happen whenever possible.

This approach will usually be easiest to arrange when the filmmaker – or someone close to the filmmaker – already knows the potential donor. The approach can begin with a phone call asking for a meeting. This might be followed up with a packet of information sent by mail or e-mail so that the donor has some time to look at and reflect on the project.

When the meeting does take place, it might be in an office, at a restaurant, at the donor's home, or at the filmmaker's loft or edit suite. When you can control the meeting place, try to keep it away from an office where your potential donor will have too many distractions. If the filmmaker is very shy and inexperienced at asking for money, then it would be smart to have a seasoned "buddy" along to help out. Find someone who is very comfortable asking for money, who is very knowledgeable about the project, and who will be respected by the donor. If the meeting is at a restaurant, the filmmaker must be prepared to pay for the meal. Scope out the restaurant before the appointment, and make sure seating will be at a table where there is a minimum of noise and other distractions. Before the meeting, be sure to have all your research ready about the donor, practice making the ask with a friend, and think about what would be the most appropriate way to dress.

The rhythm and science of making the ask is fairly simple:

- **Break the ice.** Take a few minutes just to have some introductory social conversation. Do not spend too much time chitchatting, however, because it is considered unprofessional. The donor is very aware of the purpose of the meeting and her time is precious.

- **Make your pitch.** Go ahead and pitch the project. Be brief and invite the donor to engage in a dialogue. Ideally, the donor will have many questions. Learn how to listen to the donor so you can pick up on likes and dislikes, and potential stumbling blocks to getting support.

- **Make a specific ask.** At some point it will be clear that the donor does not have any more questions, and that there is no more need to explain or describe the film. Now it is time to make a specific request for support. Here is what to do. Look the donor directly in the eyes, ask for a specific amount of money, and say how it will be used. This approach might sound something like: "Well, if you don't have any more questions, then we both know why I am here today. I hope that you can make a donation of $7,500 to my project to help with the completion editing phase of the film."

- **Shut up.** There is a simple and powerful rule-of-thumb in the fundraising world: *After the ask, the first person to talk loses!* The best thing to do after the direct ask for support is simply to shut up, and to remain completely silent until the donor says something. Let the donor make the next move, no matter how long that silence may last. This can be a difficult moment for the filmmaker who, as the silence progresses, feels more and more uncomfortable and wants to interject with an apology. That would be a mistake. Sooner or later the donor is going to say something.

- **Respond.** After the donor says something it will be the filmmaker's chance to respond. That response depends on which of three directions the donor has chosen to take:

  1. *Acceptance.* If the donor says "Yes, I'll be happy to give you that donation," then be sure to say thanks and to find out: when and how to get the donation, what type of receipt the donor needs for tax purposes, and if the donor would like to receive recognition or would prefer to remain anonymous.

  2. *Stall.* If the donor says "Maybe – let me have some more time to think about this," then find out if more information needs to be provided, and how much time the donor needs before being contacted again. Be sure to contact the donor again at the specified time/date.

3. *Rejection.* If the donor says "I'm sorry, I'm not going to be able to help you out this year," then express your thanks for the time she took to hear the request, and politely ask if it is possible for her to tell you a bit more about why she could not support the project. A lot can be learned from a rejection if it is fully explained.

Every contact with a donor should be followed up with a thank-you note or an e-mail of some sort. Remember, fundraising is also community building – it is a way to help shore up your list of contacts that can make a difference to your career and to future films. Even a rejection from a donor can have an upside if the filmmaker has made a positive impression. As the project progresses, be sure to keep everyone contacted in the loop (including people who have said "no") through regular e-mails, newsletters, or press releases.

One of my clients keeps meticulous records of everyone who has ever given her a donation. She sends out a quarterly newsletter to keep everyone informed of her current project. Then, at the end of every year, she sends out a "Year-End Wrap Up" that includes a form giving the opportunity to provide more support. She always gets a great response that includes donations from new people who received a copy of her note from a friend.

Fundraising Houseparties

I am not a fan of employing special events as ways to raise money for film projects – events where an admission fee is charged to a dinner, a benefit screening, an auction, or a concert. These types of events take a tremendous amount of energy and planning, involve large sets of people, often cost a great deal, and have the potential to end up losing money. My only exception to the rule of avoiding these is when the filmmaker: a) has a trusted set of volunteers in place who will take care of all the arrangements, and b) when all the costs are guaranteed and there is absolutely no chance of losing money (e.g., there is a corporate sponsor or all expenses are donated by the restaurant and entertainers).

What I do like is the fundraising houseparty. This is a wonderfully versatile form of fundraising appropriate for most projects. No one is charged admission to the party. People know when they are invited that if they come to the event they will be asked for support. These types of parties are great for generating support in the $3,000 to $7,000 range — although I have seen them garner much less when done in grassroots community settings, and much more when very wealthy individuals are involved. Another great advantage to this type of fundraising is that the filmmaker does not make the ask! That job is left to someone else who is a peer of those attending.

The first job is to find a supporter who is willing to donate his home or apartment to host an evening event, and who is also willing to invite friends and acquaintances. The filmmaker and host create an invitation that is sent out to a list of people three or four times larger than the number hoped for at the party. Because the invitation makes it clear that this is a fundraising event, many people will R.S.V.P. "no." But that is just fine, because those people who do decide to come have given their permission to be asked and are highly likely to give support.

The event itself should follow an agenda that will help maximize the likelihood of getting donations. Let people arrive and mingle for a while. Then sit everyone down for a formal presentation that includes: the host welcomes everyone; the filmmaker shows a short and, if possible, emotionally engaging sample from the film, followed by a question and answer period; a peer who is well known and respected by the attendees stands up and makes a lucid and direct ask for money; people are allowed time to fill out a pledge card or write checks and use credit cards.

It is important after one of these parties to contact anyone who did not give support that night, but who did not say "No, I'm not interested in providing support at this time," on their pledge card. Follow-up calls to people who fit this "maybe" category will usually garner an additional 30% more in donations.

For a very detailed explanation of this form of fundraising, along with sample invitations, refer to my book *The Fundraising Houseparty: How To Get Charitable Donations From Individuals In A Houseparty Setting.*[1]

Letters
There are whole categories of individuals who are easier to contact in writing than in person. The methods available to the filmmaker include letter writing campaigns to a small group of donors, direct mail campaigns to large numbers of people, and e-mail letter appeals.

Whatever method chosen, there are a few rules that apply across-the-board to making any form of written approach to individual donors:

- **Keep the content emotion-and-story-driven.** Try to capture the hearts of the reader and do not worry too much about facts or logic. This will not be true in other fundraising venues — with private foundations, for instance — but with individuals it is best to concentrate on involvement at an emotional level.

- **Personalize the appeal.** By "personalize" I mean see if there is a way to make the letter less generic by having it come directly from someone the donor already knows, or by having a friend of the donor at least place a short note at the bottom of the appeal letter. Personalizing the appeal will greatly increase the rate of donations, often by 50%.

- **Write a postscript.** Studies of direct mail appeals show that readers often go to the end of the letter first! It is a smart idea to include a P.S. in every appeal letter, and to make sure that the P.S. contains the central nugget of what is being said in the letter.

- **Make it easy to give.** Make it easy for the donor to respond and to make a donation. Tell the donor who to make the

---

[1] Ordering information can be found on my Web site, *www.warshawski.com*

check out to, and enclose a self-addressed return envelope (with or without a stamp). If possible, let donors use a credit card, and allow people the opportunity to volunteer to give you types of support other than money.

One of my clients received a donation from an individual for $4,000. The filmmaker asked the donor if he would be willing to write his friends and ask them for donations. The donor said "sure" but also indicated that he would not know what to say in the letter. The filmmaker offered to write the letter, which the donor then had reproduced on his own stationery. The donor sent the letter out to twelve friends, personally signed each with a short note at the bottom that said something like "Joe, I hope you can help out — this is a great project!" A few weeks later the filmmaker received three more donations of $4,000 each. Small letter writing campaigns can be quite effective when they follow a peer-to-peer scenario.

Large direct mail campaigns are much harder to predict, and they can be a very risky endeavor. To make these campaigns work, the filmmaker needs a dynamite appeal letter — ideally written by a professional direct mail marketer — and an excellent mailing list. Because the letter will go to hundreds or even thousands of recipients, the costs (labels, photocopying, postage) can be quite high, so it is easy to lose money on this type of appeal. If direct mail looks like a route to take, then try to involve a professional, get photocopying donated if possible, and be sure to get mailing label lists that have a very high likelihood of being current and appropriate for the project. One way around the cost of distribution is for the filmmaker to find a newsletter or magazine that likes the project so much they are willing to include a one page appeal in one of their mailings. For an example of an excellent direct mail appeal, take a look at the following letter sent to me by Lily Tomlin on behalf of Rob Epstein and Jeffrey Friedman's documentary *The Celluloid Closet*:

LILY TOMLIN

Holidays, 1992

Dear friend,

I am writing to ask you to help me raise money to make a film of Vito Russo's book **The Celluloid Closet**, to be directed and prduced by Academy Award winners Rob Epstein (*The Times of Harvey Milk* and *Common Threads: Stories from the Quilt*) and Jeffrey Friedman (*Common Threads*).

If you were fortunate enough to have attended one of Vito's presentations of **The Celluloid Closet** or to have read the book, then you probably recognize how important it is to preserve Vito's work for generations to come.

In the eleven years since it was first published, **The Celluloid Closet** has become the seminal reference on how lesbians and gay men have been depicted by Hollywood — from the first days of "motion pictures" right through to the 1980s.

Vito's fascinating research showed the gay and lesbian community and the entire entertainment industry how phenomenally powerful Hollywood's influence has been in shaping how gay people are viewed by society and by themselves.

Vito died of AIDS on November 7, 1990. Even though he is no longer here, we continue to need his message.

The Celluloid Closet is only one book, but it speaks volumes about discrimination, prejudice and the immense power of media stereotyping. It laid critical groundwork for the growing support for gay and lesbian rights in the entertainment industry.

Imagine how powerful **The Celluloid Closet** would be on film! Shown to millions of people through television... in theatres...

Other side, please...

REFLECTIVE IMAGE (A NOT-FOR-PROFIT 501 (C) 3 CORPORATION) 347 DOLORES STREET, #307, SAN FRANCISCO, CA 94110 schools... film festivals and forums around the world. Educating. Inspiring. Creating change.

Vito had many friends and we mourned his death and our loss. But the greatest tragedy of Vito's death was the loss for gay men, lesbians and defenders of civil liberties everywhere who looked to him as the hero he was.

From his early days, in the 1960s with the Gay Activists Alliance at the old firehouse in New York, to co-founding ACT UP and GLAAD (Gay and Lesbian Alliance Against Defamation) to his final days fighting for his own life, Vito was always, always, always at the forefront of the battle for justice.

His activism inspired thousands, including me. His dedication was matched by very few. During times when it was difficult to have faith in "leaders" it was always easy and comforting to have faith in Vito.

Vito had an extraordinary ability to see clearly how homophobia was so destructive to everyone, and how the movies were fundamental to creating contemporary homophobic stereotypes.

But to understand why I, along with other friends of Vito's, am so determined to make this film happen, one must understand that Vito was special as a person as well as an *activist*.

Vito was my precious friend for nearly 20 years. We laughed, cried and mourned with each other through our careers, politics, romances, and life's ups and downs.

Whenever anything really bad or really good would happen, there would always be a message on my answering machine from "Edith Ann." Vito could do her better than I could.

I miss him every day.

When I was thinking about how to frame this request for your help, I began to reread some of the letters Vito had written to me, back in the 1970s. Fourteen years ago, Vito wrote to warn me of:

Next page, please...

"...a larger and threatening movement against people who are different in any way... (they want) to put us back in the closet so that their children won't be influenced by positive role models. They want us to hide so they can play out their illusion in comfort..."

Sadly, what Vito wrote is as relevant today as it was in 1978. How typical of Vito to be 14 years ahead of the times... to see and understand what we must face to create a more accepting society.

That's why I hope you will be one of the very first to say *"YES... Vito's work is important. I want to help produce the film"* by sending in the most generous gift you can, right away.

This is already much more than a good idea. As you read this letter, some of the most highly acclaimed filmmaking professionals in the nation are working to bring **The Celluloid Closet** to life:

★ *Two time Oscar winner Rob Epstein and partner Jeffrey Friedman, who together conceived and directed* **Common Threads: Stories from the Quilt**, *are creating the storyboards, securing rights to filmclips and editing interviews taped with Vito before his death.*

★ *Howard Rosenman, who produced* **Father of the Bride, Shining Through** *and* **Stranger Among Us**, *and executive produced* **Common Threads**, *is executive producing* **The Celluloid Closet**.

★ *The Los Angeles chapter of* **GLAAD**, *the Gay and Lesbian Alliance Against Defamation,* **Hollywood Supports**, *and other community organizations have agreed to help get the cooperation of major studios, who own the rights to most of the filmclips.*

With your help, I know that **The Celluloid Closet** film will be made as professionally as Vito would have demanded. I know Vito would be proud of all of us who helped make it possible.

Any film project requires a lot of money, and "documentary-type" films like this one are especially hard to finance. The

Other side, please....

recession, as you might guess, makes our fundraising task even tougher.

Our $800,000 budget is conservative for a film of this type, but it is still a lot of money and a huge portion of it must be raised from private individuals.

Please give whatever you can afford — whether it be $50 or $5,000 — to preserve history and to make history at the same time.

It is important that Vito's work and activism will live on.

I urge you to go to your checkbook right this moment, before you set this aside and forget, and write out the most generous check possible.

No matter how large or how small your contribution, it is 100% tax-deductible.

Thank you for honoring the work of one of the truly great heroes of our time. I hope to hear from you very soon.

Sincerely,

Lily Tomlin

P.S. No single film can reverse 75 years of Hollywood homophobia, but **The Celluloid Closet** can teach everyone who views it how damaging homophobic stereotypes are for **all** of our society. Please... I urge you to take a moment right now to contribute as generously as you are able. Thank you.

P.P.S. I've written you hoping you will support making a film of **The Celluloid Closet**. But even if you can't help, I hope you will enjoy remembering what a special person Vito was, and how much he meant to so many friends, through the poster I've enclosed.

One other avenue for letter campaigns is open to the filmmaker: e-mail. The Internet provides a powerful way to access individual donors. E-mail reaches people instantaneously, and there is no postage cost for delivery! It costs just as much to reach thousands of people as it does to reach just one person. The great roadblock to e-mail fundraising is that the filmmaker has to avoid the appearance of sending spam — junk e-mail. There is much more ill will and anger generated by spam e-mail than by paper junk mail sent through the post office. Here are some general rules that will help make an e-mail campaign successful:

- **Create a Web site.** An e-mail appeal almost always will direct the reader to a Web site where much more information can be found on the film and the filmmaker, and where there is a form that makes it easy to make a donation and/or to ask for more information. More and more filmmakers have their own Web sites, and smart filmmakers are beginning to take advantage of the Internet's capabilities for fundraising, as well as for marketing and promotion.

- **Get connected.** The best way for an e-mail appeal to be accepted by the reader is if the letter is coming from a trusted source. Find organizations that might have a vested interest in seeing the film succeed, and ask that they allow an announcement to go out to members on their e-mail list, and/or that mention of the film with a hyperlink be placed on their own Web site.

- **Get permission.** When using e-mail to approach new people, send each e-mail out to one person at a time, use their name and ask their permission to write back with information about your project. Promise that your note is a "one time only" mailing and that no further communication will take place unless the respondent gives permission to be contacted.

- **Be specific.** Desperate cries for general support are likely to be ineffective. Come up with specific amounts for specific parts of the project. Keep the copy short and engaging, and please check for spelling and grammar errors.

- **Be smart.** In your day-to-day correspondence, be sure to add a short tag line at the end of every e-mail you send out that says something about the new film, where people can go for more information about it, and how they can give support.

Before we leave this chapter, I want to mention one other advantage to pursuing individual donations: morale. I said earlier that individual donations usually arrive in small and modest amounts, and that they tend to trickle in intermittently, especially if any type of letter writing campaign is taking place. The upside is that this trickle is great for the morale of the filmmaker and her team. Donations arrive in the mail at unexpected moments and are a great boost to morale, especially during periods when it is proving difficult to get support from foundations or corporations. But, the main advantages to pursuing individuals will always be that they are the fastest way to get support, they provide the largest pool of possible support, and they keep the filmmaker very connected to the community.

THE PAPER TRAIL: FOUNDATIONS AND GOVERNMENT AGENCIES

Private foundations and government agencies (I'll just say "foundations" for the rest of this chapter) require a completely different approach from that employed with individual donors. The major difference lies in the fact that organizational funders require a good deal of paperwork. Almost all will want to see a formal written proposal that goes before a panel of trustees before any money is awarded.

Grants have traditionally been an important source of support for noncommercial film projects. Even as the fortunes of these sources wax and wane with the vagaries of the economy and of politics, filmmakers will want to keep this type of support in the mix of income streams when and where appropriate. The great thing about grant support is that it typically comes in good-sized chunks (in the thousands of dollars) and that this support proves a great boon to giving the filmmaker credibility and enticing other support. Filmmakers must keep in mind, however, that attracting foundation support can be a lengthy process, and that this avenue of fundraising should be part of a long range plan.

Research
In Chapter 2 I listed the basic ways to do research on foundations and government agencies. Just like the instructions on qualifying the donor for individual donations, the rule of "research first" is true for agencies. It should be very clear by now that the principle of doing good basic and thorough research is primary to any and every type of fundraising for film.

The filmmaker's goal during research is to whittle the potential list of foundations down to the most probable candidates, and to discover as much of the following information as possible:

- What is the foundation's mission? What is its particular focus for funding this year?
- What are the deadlines for application?
- What information does the foundation expect in a full grant proposal?
- Who, and for what types of projects, has the foundation provided funding recently?
- What size of grants does the foundation like to make?
- What criteria are used for judging proposals?
- What is the name, phone number, and e-mail address of the program officer that will oversee the filmmaker's proposal?

Before hitting the books, the filmmaker has to begin thinking like a foundation program officer. This starts by understanding that very, very few foundations are interested in funding film as an art form. In 2000, here is how foundations divvied up their funds (as reported in the Foundation Center's *Foundation Giving Trends/2002*):

- Education - 25%
- Health - 21%
- Human Services - 14%
- **Arts & Culture - 12%**
- Public/Society Benefit - 11%
- Environment & Animals - 7%
- Science & Technology - 3%
- International Affairs - 3%
- Social Science - 2%
- Religion - 2%

Within the category "Arts & Culture" there are only a handful of places (10%) that want to fund films because of a devotion to film and filmmakers. The vast majority of funders fund a film primarily because it is an excellent way to get a message across about their particular area of interest that year – the environment, health, education, etc. These funders are primarily interested in how a film can benefit the public.

It is a great mistake to find the texts on foundations, jump to the subject index and look only under "film, video, media, television." Remember, foundations are funding the film not because it is a film, but in spite of the fact that it is a film! So, spend the vast majority of research time looking under the appropriate subject categories for the film being made – that's where the money is hiding.

First create a long laundry list of possibilities. Next, do a deeper layer of research on each of these possibilities. Request their annual reports and copies of their formal guidelines. Visit their Web sites. It is not uncommon to discover that some of the foundations on the list have geographic limitations that exclude the project, or that their subject interest this year does not perfectly match the focus of the film. This process will help whittle the first long list down to something much more manageable.

Call up people and organizations that have received grants from each foundation (they will be listed in the annual reports) and ask about their experiences with the foundation, what recommendations they have for improving your chances for success, and who is the appropriate person to contact. This is the very best way to finish your research. People who have dealt recently with the foundation have the most current and accurate information possible.

Do not be dissuaded initially by foundation guidelines that say "we don't fund media." If the project feels like a very strong match for the foundation's target area of interest, then do not give up hope yet. Many films have been funded by foundations that said "we don't fund media" when they were approached in the right way by a convincing filmmaker with a very strong project and proposal.

Your Approach: It's Personal

Here is part of a letter written to me by Ralph Arlyck, independent filmmaker (*Godzilla Meets Mona Lisa, An Acquired Taste*).

———————○———————

"Phone vs. writing: I imagine you advocate as much personal contact as possible — face-to-face if feasible, phone over letters, and so on. I know the conventional wisdom about the importance of talking to people, that one has to demonstrate one's passion for the subject, the project etc., but one also has to understand one's own strengths. I can be adequate on the phone, but I'm not irresistible. I'm better in person and I'm best of all writing. (Unfortunate progression, but there it is.) So my general approach tends to be to send people the press kit and a cover letter which says that I'll be calling them in a week or so. I would say the most common response when I do call is that the material never arrived, never got to the targeted person, they've forgotten, etc. Usually I speak not to the person in question but to an assistant who says, if he/she remembers the project, that they have my application and will be getting back to me by mail. A few weeks later the rejection letter comes. I'm courteous and friendly with the administrative assistants and frequently have nice conversations with them but the eventual answer is almost always the same."

———————○———————

Ralph is typical of most filmmakers; he would love to be able to raise lots of money by submitting written proposals and avoiding making personal contact with funders. Filmmakers can, indeed, get some grants primarily or solely on the basis of a written document. However, *70% of all grants awarded in the U.S. have involved some form of personal contact!* Filmmakers who do not attempt to make personal contact with the funder are bucking the odds and not being as effective as possible. There is a favorite saying among fundraisers that goes: "People give to people." The more the filmmaker attempts and is successful at personally engaging the funder, the higher the likelihood of success in obtaining grant support.

Why is this true? For one thing, as I noted in the chapter on individual fundraising, it is just harder to say "no" to someone with whom the funder has made a connection. More important with foundations is the elusive factor of "trust." What is it that makes a foundation feel comfortable with entrusting tens of thousands of dollars to an individual filmmaker? A good written proposal, of course, helps. But funders are smart enough to know that anyone can hire a good grantwriter to grind out a proposal. The tipping point is created by the filmmaker himself. Has he made the kind of impression on the funder that convinces them that they can trust him to complete and distribute a great product? As the head of a small family foundation once said to me: "What I look for when I meet the filmmaker is that quality that makes me feel the filmmaker will walk through fire, climb mountains, and swim across oceans if need be to finish and distribute a film."

This is why, the next step after research is to call the foundation directly and speak with the appropriate program officer. Many foundations in their guidelines will suggest as the initial contact that you "...send a letter of inquiry prior to submitting a formal proposal." Whenever possible, do not make this the first form of contact — especially with foundations that say "we don't fund media" in their guidelines. It is far too easy for foundations to *pro forma* toss aside good project ideas by just sending back a standard rejection form letter that may have been signed by a secretary or receptionist on the basis of a simple instruction from the CEO that says "Don't show me any applications that have the words *film, video, media, radio,* or *television* in them."

When I conduct workshops on fundraising I encourage an informal process called "testify," which allows anyone to stand up and spontaneously testify about something they just heard that has a lot of resonance to them. During one workshop when I talked about the letter of inquiry, a young woman stood up and told the following story. A year earlier she had been working on a documentary project about a degenerative disease. One day she opened up the newspaper and noticed that the CEO of a local corporate foundation had a child with this particular disease. She was sure that he would want to support her project, so she crafted a strong letter of inquiry to his foundation even though the guidelines said, "We don't fund media." The next week she received a standard rejection form letter from the foundation. Naturally, she was disappointed. A month later, she found herself at a fancy reception and by chance ran into the CEO. During their conversation, he asked the filmmaker what projects she was working on. When she mentioned her documentary, his interest was immediately piqued. He said, "You should definitely send a proposal to my foundation. We don't normally fund media projects, but I'm sure we would give you some support." She replied, "I'm embarrassed to tell you this, but I already sent in a letter of inquiry and received a rejection note." The CEO looked her in the eye and told her he had never seen that letter of inquiry, and that she should forward a full proposal directly to his attention. Soon thereafter she received a substantial grant from the very same foundation that had previously rejected her on the basis of a letter of inquiry.

There will be times when sending a brief letter of inquiry cannot be avoided – when there is no phone or e-mail contact information for the foundation, or when the program officer just refuses to chat with you without getting paperwork first. But many foundations will have at least a short conversation with you first, if you are courteous, brief, and ask intelligent questions.

The goal of the filmmaker at this stage is to find ways to make the funder understand and like the project so much, and have such great respect for and trust in the filmmaker, that the program officer does everything in her power to help make sure the filmmaker gets support from her foundation.

Begin by calling the foundation and asking to speak with the appropriate program officer. Hopefully, the filmmaker already has the name of the right person to contact. If not, then the art of "getting past the secretary" will have to be mastered. My advice here is simple: Make the secretary love you, don't be obnoxious, and never leave more than one message if any.

Another way to get past the secretary quickly is to name-drop. If it is possible to get referred to the foundation by someone already known to them, then dropping that person's name will often get the caller through to the program officer very quickly. Be warned, however, that this tactic can only be used when the person whose name is being mentioned has given permission for the use of her name. Here is what filmmaker Julie Reichert wrote me recently: "What also seems to work like a charm is to have a name to drop. For XYZ Foundation, I called a grantee at Harvard (go to the top!) and chatted with her about her work and my work, and she was fine with my using her name in calling XYZ. I had tried previously with no success to get someone on the phone. But by using her name, I got a call back right away."

Once the appropriate program officer is reached, begin any and all conversations with a foundation by saying something that shows understanding of its current year's mission and area of focus. Here is a typical call scenario:

> *"Hello, my name is Morrie Warshawski. I understand your foundation is interested this year in issues of sustainability and saving the tropical rain forests of Brazil."*

> *"Yes, that's true. But I'm very busy, all our information is in our printed guidelines, and we prefer to receive a letter of inquiry prior to any other contacts"*

> *"Yes, I understand that. I have read all your information thoroughly, and I'm prepared to send you a letter of inquiry.*

However, I have just a couple of quick questions I wanted to ask first because they are not covered in any of your written materials."

"Well, in that case, you can have two minutes. What do you want to ask?"

Now the filmmaker must quickly and effectively pitch the project, follow up with an intelligent question, and hope to engage the funder in an interesting conversation. The funder may say, "Don't waste your time – that project has no chance with us." Or, as is often the case, the funder might say, "That sounds interesting. Tell me a little more." If the scenario goes well, the funder will invite you to submit a full proposal, and will even offer some specific suggestions to improve your chances for success.

Let's hear what a funder – Jon Jensen of the George Gund Foundation – had to say about this phone call (taken from an interview in Andy Robinson's excellent book *Grassroots Grants: An Activist's Guide to Proposal Writing*):

———————○———————

Call foundation staff and tell them what you're doing. Give them a quick, simple description of your project — no more that 90 seconds — then ask your questions. I can think of a number of proposals I would have declined to support without first having had a phone conversation and forming a positive opinion about the person on the other end of the line...If you get me on the phone you get five times as much information as we list in our guidelines. This is by design: we want to be responsive, not prescriptive. My job is to demystify the process — I tell you everything I can at every stage of the game. I can also help you identify the strengths and weaknesses of your proposal and the obstacles you'll need to overcome if you want to get funded...Foundation-wise applicants know how to time the asking of the key question: "What are our chances of getting a grant?" It is often an unasked question because the applicant doesn't want to hear the answer. If asked at the appropriate time, however, this question can save the grantseeker a great deal of time, labor, and anxiety.

———————————○———————————

It is instructive to keep in mind the types of things that foundations worry about, and the criteria they apply to judging a media proposal. Here is a sample list of criteria provided to program officers from an actual foundation that funds media regularly:

XYZ FOUNDATION'S 10 BASIC QUESTIONS FOR EVALUATING A VIDEO/TELEVISION PROPOSAL

1. What is the purpose/goal of this project?
2. Does the purpose of this project fall within the guidelines of my program?
3. Is the medium of video/television an effective way to reach the goal?
4. Is video/television a cost effective way to reach the goal?
5. Is the proposing organization capable of producing or overseeing the production of a video?
6. How will the video be used? Who is the intended audience?
7. How will it be marketed/promoted/advertised/distributed?
8. What uses other than broadcast will be made of the video?
9. Are there related materials that support the video?
10. Is the budget reasonable? Is the schedule realistic?

Before moving on to writing the proposal, let's hear what one more funder had to say about what things the foundation thinks about when scanning a filmmaker's proposal (taken from an interview with the Playboy Foundation in the December 2000 issue of *The Independent*):

———————○———————

First I look at the paperwork: Will the subject matter advance or promote the Foundation's mission? What is the filmmaker's experience in making films and raising money? Who are the other funders? Can the filmmaker raise enough money or find enough backers to see the project through to completion? What is the distribution plan? Who is its intended audience? Is there a fiscal sponsor? etc. Then I sit down and look at the trailer or rough cut: How does it look? Does it do what the filmmaker intended? Will the Foundation be proud to have its name associated with the project? If the answers are in the affirmative to most of these questions, we usually award it a grant. I only compare one film to another when a project has been done before. Then I ask myself, what makes this one different or better?

———————○———————

Writing the Proposal

Now, finally, the grant can be written. There are stacks of books available on the art of grantwriting. What I hope the reader has understood by now is that the written proposal is just the tip of the iceberg. If the filmmaker has followed all of my instructions up until now, then the act of creating the grant should be a simple matter of pulling together many elements that are already in place, and creating just a few more items we have not yet discussed. The filmmaker with strong writing skills can create the entire document himself, and then call on a colleague to give it a once-over. The filmmaker with poor-to-average writing skills will have to work with a partner, or hire a professional grantwriter for assistance.

There are a few general rules that apply to almost any type of grantwriting. First, be sure to find out exactly what the funder wants to see. Most funders have specific guidelines that ask for information of a certain type, and usually of a certain length. *Always follow the guidelines of the funder!* If the filmmaker wants to alter the guidelines by adding more information, or additional types of support materials, then the rule is to ask permission from the funder first. Otherwise, only send what is requested in the format and length the funder has enumerated.

Next, keep some stylistic rules in mind. Make the prose of the grant as simple and direct as possible. Stay away from very long convoluted sentences with many dependent clauses. Use plain English, and employ as many bullets or subheads as necessary to help organize the proposal and make it easy for funders to find any bit of information they want at a moment's notice; or, as the saying goes, "Can't scan it? Can it!" Another important principle is to strike a balance between mind and heart, reason and passion. When writing letters to individual donors I counseled erring toward the side of passion – to make the letters as heartfelt and emotional as possible. That would be a mistake with foundations. In this arena the proposal must convince the funder that the filmmaker is both passionately committed to the project and a credible and levelheaded person who can be trusted to create a quality program. Show too much passion and lose the funder's respect. Show too much intellect without any passion, and the funder begins to wonder about your power to stay-the-course when the going gets tough.

With respect to producing the document, never put your information on fancy colored or textured paper, and never use expensive bindings or covers — funders frown on this since it is considered a waste of money. Keep in mind that the funder may have to take the proposal apart as soon as it is received and make multiple copies for the Board of Trustees. Use plain white paper (8 1/2" x 11" only — never any larger) and a plain font 12 pt. typeface (Times Roman, Book Antiqua, Garamond, Arial, and Courier are quite common). Smaller type may get more information on each page, but that makes the writing much harder to read — especially for any funder who is farsighted. I actually heard a trustee say once that he rejected a grant because it was just too hard to read the words on the page. Some funders will allow transmission of a proposal by e-mail; if that's the case, be sure the software formats for text and attachments are compatible.

Elements of a Full Grant Proposal
Because every proposal is going to be different, and tailored specifically for each funder, there is no one standard format that will suffice. However, I like to have my clients pull together in advance everything they might ever need so that they are ready for any and every proposal scenario.

Here is an outline of what I consider a full grant proposal:

1. COVER LETTER
2. TITLE PAGE
3. TABLE OF CONTENTS
4. FORMAL REQUEST
5. DESCRIPTION OF THE PROJECT
6. STATEMENT PROVING NEED
7. DESCRIPTION OF INTENDED AUDIENCE
8. WHY I BECAME INVOLVED WITH THIS PROJECT
9. TREATMENT
10. PRODUCTION PLANS & TIMELINE
11. PERSONNEL
12. DISTRIBUTION AND COMMUNITY OUTREACH PLANS
13. EVALUATION PLAN

14. FUNDING STRATEGY FOR COMPLETION OF PROJECT
15. BUDGETS
16. MISCELLANEOUS SUPPORT MATERIALS
    i) FISCAL SPONSOR LETTER
    ii) LETTERS OF SUPPORT
    iii) LETTERS OF COMMITMENT
    iv) PRESS CLIPPINGS
    v) FULL RESUMES OF PERSONNEL
    vi) PROMO CLIP OR SAMPLE REEL

Let's take a look at each of these elements to gain a bit more clarity on what the filmmaker needs to produce to make each section credible.

- **Cover Letter**. Very simply, the filmmaker writes a one page introductory note on letterhead, and reminds the funder of their previous conversations. The filmmaker will want to say here how much money is being requested and for what the funds will be used. Thank the funder for accepting the proposal for consideration. Offer to be available to answer any questions that might come up. Be sure to say, "I will be calling in a few days just to make sure this package arrived safely and to see if you might have any questions you'd like to ask me before the proposal goes to panel." If other funders have already given to the project, be sure to mention that in this cover note. And, include a P.S. that reiterates some important point.

- **Title Page**. Keep it simple. Don't forget to include all necessary contact information including name, address, phone, fax, e-mail and Web address. It is good to place under the title of the film, its intended length and format and, possibly, the major audience for whom the film is intended. If an image has been chosen to represent the film, it can be placed here as well.

- **Table of Contents.** This is necessary only if the proposal is fairly lengthy, for it helps funders find sections easily.

- **Formal Request.** This is your introductory paragraph that quickly describes the project, the portion of the project for which you want support (e.g., script development and writing, editing, community outreach, etc.), and the exact amount of money you want. *Be sure that the amount of the request has been cleared with the funder before writing the proposal.* This will be the last call made to the program officer before writing the grant. The filmmaker should, through research, already have discovered what the funder's comfort zone of giving is. But, things change and the only way to know if the funder still gives out a certain size grant is to ask directly. I would call my contact at the foundation just before submitting the proposal and say: "I'm glad you have agreed to allow me to send in a full proposal and I'm almost ready to finish my document. I'm calling just to make sure that the foundation will be comfortable with my request for $13,000." If you have a good relationship with the program officer, then you will probably get an honest answer that either confirms that this amount is still doable, or that suggests a lower or even higher request. Many a grant request to a foundation has been won or lost just on the basis of the amount of the request.

- **Description of the Project.** Here the filmmaker can spend more time explaining what the project is about, the approach that will be taken, what topics will be covered and in what depth, and the intended outcome.

- **Statement Proving Need.** This is where the filmmaker takes as much time and space as necessary to prove that the world needs this program. This is a good place to mention a few other programs that have already been made about the same topic, or in the same genre, and to differentiate your program.

- **Description of Intended Audience.** Give a good laundry list of all the audiences for whom this project is being made.

Provide demographic and psychographic information about whom you want to reach.

- **Why I Became Involved with This Project.** A very brief – one or two sentences – explanation of how and why the filmmaker became involved with this project. This helps personalize the proposal, and answers any question the funder might have about the filmmaker's connection to the topic.

- **Treatment.** For many funders, the treatment will be one of the most important sections of the entire proposal. I have had a number of funders tell me that this is where filmmakers often completely miss the mark. A treatment is very different from the description of the project earlier in the proposal. Instead, the treatment is literally a written depiction of exactly what will be seen in the project if a viewer were sitting in front of a screen – scene by scene. Everything in the treatment is visual, and there is no explanation of themes or intent. The formula the treatment follows is: "First we see... and then we see... and next we see...." Unless the funder says otherwise, try to keep the treatment to a length of two single-spaced pages.

Here is a segment of a treatment for the film *A Midwife's Life: Discovering the Life of Martha Ballard*, by Laurie Kahn-Leavitt, which is reprinted from a full grant proposal with permission from the National Endowment for the Humanities:

———————————————◯———————————————

It is the middle of the night. We are close on the face of a woman. It is streaked with sweat. The scene is claustrophobic, with faces, objects crowding the frame. The woman is groaning. The visual palette includes many rich shades of brown, lit by flickering yellow and red from the firelight. It is dark. We can almost smell the burning wood and the steam rising from the kettle in the fireplace. The presence of people in the room is magnified by long shadows cast against the unpainted wood walls of the house. We hear the voices of women talking, soothing the woman in labor, and the camera pulls back to reveal a scene filled with women — with their hands, shoulders, plain blouses, skirts. The woman in labor is not lying on a bed, but is squatting, in the final moments of childbirth, held in the arms of three other women. One rather older, somewhat stout, but strong woman is obviously in charge. Her face is plain, but the lines on her face and the look in her eyes reveal depth of character. She is giving instructions to the other women to get hot compresses, to rub the woman's lower back, to apply a specific herbal ointment. As she soothes and encourages the woman in labor, as the woman in labor pants and catches her breath, we hear the voice of the midwife reading an entry from her diary:

I was Calld to Capt Sualls wife in Travail I crost on the ice. Got there at 70 Clock Evenng. Mrs Sewalls neighbors were caild to her assistance. It was a very Cold night.

The midwife in charge leans over. And then we hear a loud baby's cry.

Mrs Sewall was safe delivered at 1 this morn of a fine daghter. May God long preserv her. I sett up with my Patients.

As the baby is cleaned off, wrapped, and eased into a wooden cradle, Tabitha Sewall names her daughter Elizabeth. She lies back in bed, exhausted from her nine-hour labor. The midwife and the three women who have helped out are drowsy. They lean back toward the kitchen fire, the midnight cold at their backs, small clouds of mist above their whispers.

———————————○———————————

- **Production Plans & Timeline.** Let the funder know where and when the project will be undertaken and what difficulties might be encountered. Place here a generic timeline for creating the film and taking it into distribution (as discussed in Chapter 3).

- **Personnel.** Provide brief, one-paragraph descriptions of each of the key personnel (yourself, the director, cinematographer, editor, advisors, etc.). Make sure everyone sounds credible, and be sure to mention major accomplishments and any significant awards.

- **Distribution and Community Outreach Plans.** Describe all conceivable ways this program will reach its audience. This section must be very convincing. It must show that the filmmaker has really thought about and researched the various avenues of distribution. More and more, funders are interested in also seeing a community outreach plan — something that shows the filmmaker is concerned with partnerships that will help get the word out about the film and that will give added value to any broadcast. Many filmmakers will want to create a Web site for their projects. This is the part of the proposal where that Web site and how it extends the project can be described.

Here is the distribution plan that the producers at WGBH submitted with their application to the National Endowment for the Humanities (reprinted with permission of the NEH) for their documentary *MacArthur*:

———————○———————

"MacArthur" will be broadcast nationally on PBS as a part of the historical documentary series *The American Experience*. WGBH's National Promotion staff has an impressive track record of placements for the series we produce and publicize: in fall 1996, for example, our efforts for October premieres alone generated almost 30,000 column inches of coverage nationwide, reaching a cumulative audience of 1.3 billion readers, and representing an ad equivalency of nearly $3 million.

To promote "MacArthur," *The American Experience* will coordinate radio interviews and do an extended mailing to television critics and reviewers. In addition to these traditional methods, WGBH's National Promotion team will take advantage of emerging technology to explore new ways to reach a wider audience. PBS Express, our proprietary online communication system with PBS and the 300+ public television stations nationwide, allows us to alert the individual stations concerning opportunities to expand their promotion efforts.

An enhanced Web site, similar to those developed for programs broadcast recently, containing timelines, a bibliography, real audio interviews with scholars and on-camera witnesses is planned. *The American Experience* sees its home page on the World Wide Web

(*http://www.wgbh.org/AmericanExperience*) as an educational resource, providing additional material to
viewers and schools, and a promotional tool, a new
way to reach beyond the traditional public television
audience. Students regularly turn to this Web site for
research assistance; it has also become an important
vehicle for viewer response.

"MacArthur" will be made available for audiovisual
and home video distribution. Three-year PBS broadcast rights will be renewed indefinitely. Programs
from *The American Experience* have become favorites
among teachers of history and social studies because
they are now the standard against which any history
documentary is measured. More tellingly, they are
very popular among students from junior high school
through college because they are superb examples of
the storyteller's art.

Beyond the classroom and home video market, these
films are frequently purchased by local libraries and
made part of their permanent collection. Also, many
of *The American Experience* programs have been distributed in Europe. "MacArthur" will be marketed in
the same way.

————————————◯————————————

- **Evaluation Plan.** The question of evaluation comes up because
  most of the projects that foundations support have clearly
  defined and quantifiable outcomes. Funders are increasingly
  sensitive to finding ways to measure the success of their funding efforts. Therefore, the question of evaluation is likely to
  come up and the filmmaker should be ready with an answer.

For many media projects the question may seem whimsical. How, for instance, can success be measured for a short experimental film, or for a dramatic feature that is meant to give people pleasure? Filmmakers need to be creative here and say they will make use of any or all of the following methods for evaluation:

- Measuring critical response in the media
- Response from specialists in the field
- Awards won at festivals
- Total number of sales in all intended markets
- Focus group opinions
- Evaluations from users
- Changes in behavior of the intended audience
- Amount of matching funds from various sources

- **Funding Strategy For Completion Of Project.** Because most funders cannot provide full funding for a film project, there will be a portion of the budget that still must be raised over and above the request being made. Every funder will want to know how the filmmaker plans to raise the rest of the money. The key to providing a good answer is for the filmmaker to play "what if" and create a fundraising plan/strategy that actually sounds practical for the project. Here is a sample of how a strategy might look:

"We are requesting $50,000 from your foundation to begin production on our film *The Warshawski Family Diaries*, which has a total budget of $500,000. Should your foundation provide start-up costs, we plan to raise the remaining $450,000 in the following manner: 50% ($225,000) from donations from four or five private foundations and government agencies; 10% ($45,000) in pre-sales to foreign television; 20% ($90,000) from individuals through direct mail campaigns and fundraising houseparties; and 20% ($90,000) from corporate sponsors for a national airing on PBS."

- Budgets. I recommend having the following budgets ready to go:

  - A one-page budget summary that shows the major headings and subtotals
  - A complete budget for the entire project that shows detail for every expense and is heavily annotated with as many budget notes as necessary
  - Separate detailed budgets for various "projects" – those portions of the entire film for which you are planning to request support (e.g., script development, community outreach, postproduction, etc.)

- **Fiscal Sponsor Letter.** Funders will need to see a copy of the fiscal sponsor's official 501(c)(3) letter provided by the IRS, which proves their nonprofit status. In addition to this, ask the fiscal sponsor to write an enthusiastic "to whom it may concern" cover letter that explains why they decided to sponsor the project, and why they feel it is important that funders provide support. Also keep on file brochures and promotional materials about the fiscal sponsor just in case the sponsor might be unfamiliar to the funder.

- **Letters Of Support.** Garnering letters of support should be a part of every filmmaker's modus operandi. These letters are especially important in helping to gain credibility for a filmmaker and a project when asking for grants. Start getting letters as soon as possible from:

  - Professional associations and experts in the topic area of the film
  - Other well-known and well-respected filmmakers in the genre of the film
  - Distributors (these are the strongest letters that can be attached to a grant)

- Broadcasters
- Potential end-users

Make sure the letter is written on letterhead stationery, contains no typos, and is signed. Do not be surprised if a potential supporter when asked for a letter says: "I'm happy to give you a letter, but I'm not sure what to say. Would you mind writing it for me and I'll have it typed up on my stationery?" I love it when I am asked to write my own letter of reference because now I can be sure to get the exact letter I want and need.

- **Letters Of Commitment.** Keep these on file to keep yourself safe. Make sure that anyone and everyone mentioned by name in the proposal as a participant in the film has written an official note for the files that confirms commitment to the project. This is especially important when well-known people are being attached to a project. Funders will want to know that the filmmaker is not just name-dropping.

- **Press Clippings.** Generate as much press coverage as possible about both the project and the production team. Press clippings are a great boon to the credibility of the filmmaker – even if the source is a hometown newspaper. Clippings help lay the groundwork for fundraising by raising awareness of the project and helping to generate "buzz." Learn the fine art of photocopying and make sure that all press clippings meet the following criteria:

  - Clean, crisp, legible copies
  - Original size copies (never reduce the clipping to a smaller type size)
  - Longer articles are cut up and laid out on a series of 8 1/2" x 11" sheets of plain white paper
  - Each clipping contains a contact name and address
  - Each clipping provides the name of the original source, date of publication, and page numbers

If the mention of the team and the project are just a small

part of a larger article, then excerpt just that portion, or high-light that part with a marker, or bring attention to that por-tion by increasing its size and placing the drawing of a mag-nifying glass around it.

- **Full Resumes of Personnel.** Have all team members and advisors provide a full resume to keep on file. These can be excerpted for use in grants. Occasionally a funder will want to see a full resume.

- **Promo Clip or Sample Reel.** It is possible to begin a project and not have a promo clip of the intended work. However, once some funds have been accrued, and some shooting has taken place, many funders will request a look at some work in progress that represents the tenor of the film and shows the skills of the team. The sample reel does not have to be long – anything from five to twelve minutes is usually enough. I do not recommend longer samples because it shows the funder too much, and leaves open too many opportunities to make mistakes and/or trigger too many new questions. Short and sweet is just fine.

Having said that, I do have two other criteria for the effective fundraising clip. The first is that the content of the clip should (ideally) be very representative of the style and content of the intended finished film, and that it should be very engaging. The clip should make the viewer want to see more.

My second criterion is one that filmmakers do not like to hear – the clip should be as technically "clean" and free of problems (sound and image) as possible. Funders – even very seasoned and media savvy ones – have difficulty seeing beyond techni-cal difficulties in a tape. This means that the filmmaker is going to have to spend some time and money creating a good clean copy of some material. Do not think that an explanatory note can be attached to a tape and that that will take care of any problems. Here is a sample of an actual note that a film-maker sent me to accompany a sample reel:

PLEASE NOTE that the material found on this tape consists of excerpted scenes, not examples of completed work. As such, it is important to keep in mind several things while viewing:

- You are viewing a 16mm film work print that has been transferred to videotape. In the final version, the color will be corrected and a clean print created.
- The narration you hear is *temporary* and rough, and is read by an amateur. The final narration will emphasize goal-action-results messages and will refer to specific principles of creating community change. In the final version it will be read by a professional narrator.
- Scenes do not flow as smoothly as they will in the final version. Some shots will be replaced.
- The sounds levels are uneven. Voices will be much clearer in final version. Scenes with no sound at all will be filled with sound effects or music. The music is also temporary, although evocative of what we intend.
- At this stage, there are no titles or name identifiers for the people speaking.

If the work sample needs to have this type of note attached to it, then the video is not ready to be sent out at all. These notes are rarely read by funders, and when they are read are often ignored the moment an image comes on the screen.

Occasionally the filmmaker will not have new material to submit from the intended project, and may want to create a sample reel of past work. This work might also include samples from completed pieces by other team members (especially the cinematographer and the editor). In this case, try to include works that are as similar to the intended project as possible. It would be a mistake, for instance, to submit a verité documentary sample for a dramatic narrative feature proposal.

One last instruction is to only send a sample when a funder gives permission or makes a specific request. Also submit the sample in the format the funder wants, label and package the tape appropriately, and be sure to include a self-addressed stamped envelope if return of the tape is desired.

Last Calls

Now that the proposal has been sent in (well before the official deadline) it may seem that the filmmaker's work is done. Not true. There is still one more very crucial phone call that must be made. One last window of opportunity remains for the filmmaker to help increase chances of success. A week or two after submitting the grant, call the program officer in charge of the proposal and ask if the paperwork arrived safely, if the officer has had a chance to look it over, and if there are any questions the officer would like to ask.

It is amazing how often a grant is submitted with small or even large errors. I once looked over a proposal about to be submitted to the Corporation for Public Broadcasting (CPB) for $500,000, and right on their cover page the filmmaker had made an addition error. It is not the job of the foundation to call applicants back and advise them of errors in a proposal. However, if the filmmaker makes the call to a sympathetic program officer, quite often that person will allow corrections to be made to any mistakes or any confusing narrative portions before the grant is given to the deciding panel or board of trustees. Many a grant can be won or lost as a result of this call.

The very first time I ever offered my workshop on fundraising I gave this advice to the participants: "If any of you have submitted a grant recently and it is still pending, go home and call the program officer right away to see if everything is okay." A few weeks later I got a call from a woman who attended the workshop and wanted to tell me that this suggestion was the most important thing she had learned. The day after the workshop she called the foundation where she had submitted a grant for her documentary. The program officer told her he was glad she had called because there was a section of her proposal that he did not quite understand and he wondered if she could give him a better explanation. The filmmaker described over the phone what she had meant, and the program officer replied, "Oh, that makes much more sense. Our board doesn't meet for another two weeks, so why don't you rewrite that section of the grant just as you told it to me over the phone, and I'll substitute it for what you sent me." She ended up getting the grant she requested and was certain this change had made all the difference.

Once this call is made, the rest is up to the funder. After the board of trustees meets, the funder will contact all applicants, usually in writing. Some few lucky applicants will receive a "Congratulations, You Won!" letter. When this happens, be sure to say "thank you" to the funder and to the program officer who was the main contact. A simple card or phone call will suffice. Do not forget to ask funders if they want to be formally mentioned in the film's credits and publicity (some will want to remain anonymous), and if they have a particular wording or image they prefer to have used. And, make sure to stay in touch with your funders throughout the progress of the production, to invite them to an opening screening when the film is complete, and to send them a copy of the program for their files. The funder has now become your partner and will want to be treated like a team member.

Many more applicants are going to receive a " Sorry Pardner, You Lose" rejection letter. These letters typically are written in a generalized way that goes something like:

---------------------------------○---------------------------------

"Dear Applicant: Thank you for bringing your project to our foundation for consideration. Our board of trustees has just met and it is my unfortunate task to

*have to tell you that your project was not chosen for
support this year. Although we found your project of
great interest, we are just not able to help all the fine
applicants like yourself that come to our foundation
for assistance each year. We wish you the best of
luck with your endeavors, and invite you to apply to
us again in the future should you have a project that
closely matches our guidelines."*

———————————○———————————

These rejection letters rarely if ever tell the specific reasons for rejection. Therefore, the filmmaker still has one more call to make. Make
sure the anger and depression caused by rejection has subsided
before making this call. Then pick up the phone and contact the program officer at the foundation. Be very polite. Thank the foundation
for having taken time to consider the application you sent. Then
directly ask the program officer if she could be kind enough to provide
a little more detail on the discussion that took place during the consideration of the proposal, and if there is any important
information that she can give you about the reasons for being
rejected. Never ever get angry with the funder, or berate them for not
giving support.

I remember once giving this advice to a filmmaker who immediately
said, "I tried that once and it didn't work!" I asked him to explain what
happened and he said, "Well, I got a standard rejection letter from a
foundation that really should have given me a grant and I was really
pissed. My film was exactly within their mission and guidelines and
they had no good reason for rejecting me. So I called up the program
officer at the foundation and complained. I told her that they were
wrong not to give me the grant, and that they obviously had not
looked at it closely, and that I wanted to send it back to them so they
could reconsider." This is a perfect example of how you should *never*
talk to a funder. This filmmaker ruined his chances for ever getting a

grant from this foundation, and he tainted the waters for other film-makers as well. No one likes to get rejected, but you have to learn how to handle these rejections professionally.

If the application went to a government funder, then they must divulge notes from the panel meeting and give some good solid reasons for the rejection. Private foundation officers are not under the same obligation to divulge information, but quite often they can provide details that might be very revealing. Perhaps the filmmaker is doing something in the application that confuses funders. Or maybe the funder only said "no" because it is the end of the fiscal year and they had no funds left over. Whatever the reason, the filmmaker has to make an effort to ferret it out. Also, the filmmaker when making this call is sending a very strong signal to the funding community. That signal says: "I am serious about this endeavor. Every time I am rejected I will be making this phone call." Funders will take the film-maker more seriously, and tend to pay more attention to the next application for support.

Even with funders that have rejected a proposal, I would counsel to stay in touch. Keep them informed on the progress of the project (via press releases and newsletters), and be sure they hear about the successful completion of the film and are invited to an opening screening. This helps lay the groundwork for any future proposals. Fundraising from foundations is a long-term process, so consider any rejection a short-term loss that provides an opportunity for eventual long-term gain.

ALL THE REST

Good Housekeeping

By now it should be clear that fundraising can be a complicated affair. If a number of sources are being approached at the same time, and deadlines are looming, it can be very difficult to keep everything organized. Adopt some type of simple bookkeeping system that helps keep track of actions taken or pending, upcoming grant deadlines, and any important information that has been learned about all funders. If the filmmaker has access to database software, then that can be an excellent tool for this task.

I prefer to have two different types of information readily available. One is a **Fundraising Journal.** This can be on paper, or on a computer file. Create a separate page for each and every funder. The page will have all contact information on it. After that, every time a contact is made with the foundation, it is entered in the journal chronologically. This is especially important to do right after having a conversation with any funder, so that information just learned can be placed in the journal. I turn to this journal before making a call to any funder, so that I can remind myself of what we talked about before. Here is a typical journal page:

———————————○———————————

THE GENEROUS CHARITABLE TRUST (GCT)

P. O. Box 75444

San Anselmo, CA 94732

Ph. 415.555.9335

Fax. 415.555.9336

www.gct.org

Contact: Astoria Buckes, Media Program Director

asbuckes@gct.org

Note: Astoria only available afternoons, Tu-Fri

2/16/02: Called about Project X. Astoria says "already heavily committed to film this year" – not hopeful about my chances, but she's heard of my work and wouldn't mind meeting for lunch.

2/26/02: Nice lunch date with Astoria at Le Burger Joint. Discovered she loves veggie burgers, enjoys jogging, raised in Missouri, ex-husband is 18th Century scholar. Foundation is pretty dry right now, doesn't see much chance for Project X. BUT, she did say if I ever get a number of other funders on board, and I'm short "just a bit" she might be able to kick in some discretionary funds at her disposal.

5/1/02: Called Astoria – reminded her of our lunch and told her I'd raised $190,000 and just need $10,000 more to complete the project. She requests full packet/proposal (sent) and says call in two weeks.

5/16/02: Call to Astoria – she's not ready yet. Call back again in 2 wks.

5/26/02: Yippee! Got the dough. Check to arrive in 2 wks. Astoria says "Be sure to give Foundation recognition in all publicity and in end credits." THANK YOU note sent right away to Foundation's Board of Trustees. Bought single orchid and hand delivered to Astoria.

6/5/02: Foundation check arrives.

10/5/02: Newsletter on Project X sent to AB.

1/1/03: Invite Astoria and Foundation staff to Project X premiere at Royale – she won't take comps and insists on buying 20 tix.

2/1/03: Final report sent to Foundation, along with video copy for their files.

6/1/03: Call to Astoria re funding new project, "Return of Project X" - she's receptive (Foundation loved the first film) and says send info then, "Let's have lunch."

———————○———————

Over a few years this journal becomes a very powerful tool for fundraising. Another list I recommend is a one or two page **Summary of Proposals** that provides a very quick visual representation of all proposal activity. A typical format might be:

Date	Amt. of Rqst.	Funder	Project	Results	Notes
5/1/03	$50,000	Ford Fndtn	Production	rjctd 7/01/03	
5/10/03	$10,000	Megabucks Fund	Scripting Phase	yes! on 6/30/03	
5/25/03	$100,000	ITVS	Completion Funds	(pending)	Call DL on 7/1

Keep this on a wall, a bulletin board, or separate computer document page so that it serves as an easy reminder of what proposals are still pending. For some positive reinforcement, try highlighting in yellow or circling in red any proposals that are accepted. The only other record-keeping device should be a set of separate manila folders devoted to storing information and correspondence with each funder over the years.

Going Corporate

My clients have not had great success getting donations from large corporations that do not have a formal foundation. Most large corporations tend to shun controversy and are conservative in their funding choices. This stance eliminates alliances with many of the film topics chosen by independent filmmakers. Also, the corporate world is one fundraising environment where having connections does make a significant difference, and most independent filmmakers are not "connected."

However, it is possible to get support from corporations. The film-maker who follows this path must keep in mind one major difference between corporations and all other funders: A corporation will always want something in return for its donation, and that something is almost always exposure with a specific audience (e.g., potential or current customer for the corporation's products). This principle is often referred to as "Enlightened Self Interest" or **ESI**.

This means that in addition to the written materials required for a full grant proposal to a foundation, the filmmaker must also be prepared to be lucid on two more issues:

- **Specific demographics of the intended audience.** The corporation will want to see facts and figures for exactly whom the program will reach, where they live, and how many people will end up viewing the program in what settings. Be prepared to have this data for every market the program will enter during distribution.

- **What's in it for them.** Opportunities for exposure need to be enumerated. Where will the corporation's name/logo appear in the film, in its packaging, and in promotional materials? What kind of community outreach and marketing/p.r. will be done, and how prominent will the filmmakers display the corporation's level of involvement? Are there ways the corporation can use the program internally with its staff, or with its clients, as a promotional tool or as a perk for employees?

The corporation is going to take the figures provided, do the math (e.g., total cost of its investment divided by total number of potential viewers), and come up with a figure for how much it will cost to reach each person using the film as a vehicle. If this figure does not compare favorably with normal costs of advertising, then it will not make sense to be involved with the film.

It is not unusual to have a list of "sponsorship opportunities" with different levels of support at which the corporation receives different benefits. All this means is that when the filmmaker talks to the corporation, the conversation has a different tone and flavor to it than the conversation with a foundation program officer or an individual donor. The filmmaker has to be prepared to convince the corporation that the film is a great marketing opportunity and an excellent vehicle for gaining goodwill in the community or in the work place.

There are exceptions to these rules for corporations. Funding at a corporation is very personality based – and that personality is generally whoever is running the business. When a CEO has a personal interest in a topic or in a filmmaker, then a donation can be made on that basis alone. Filmmaker Jon Else, for instance, was able to get support from The Gap for his documentary *Cadillac Desert* because "...the guy who owns The Gap is a resolute environmentalist ... he's also a guy who's very resolute about giving something back to the community." (*RealScreen*, January 1998). It is a smart idea to keep up on CEOs by reading the business sections and society columns of newspapers. If you discover a corporate leader who has shown some personal interest in the same topic as your film, then anything can happen. The trick will be to reach that person, ideally through finding an intermediary who can open the door for you, or at the very least through writing.

Ann Telfer, Director of *In Love and In Danger: A Documentary on Dating Violence*, literally ran into her connection to the corporation Parke-Davis (now Pfizer) on the track at a recreation center in Ann Arbor, Michigan. Her running mate, whose husband was the Chief Financial Officer at Parke-Davis, helped open the door to a meeting with the Vice President of the Human Resources Department, and this resulted in a $30,000 donation. Telfer had done her research and knew something about the VP, as well as what the HR Department does. She pitched her project emphasizing the angle of domestic violence and the work force – an issue of interest to Parke-Davis. After this initial donation, Telfer maintained an eight-year relation, with lots of dialogue, that resulted in funding for a second tape, as well as a donation to fund a Dating and Domestic Violence Prevention Endowment.

The Corner Store

Small businesses can be an excellent source of support, especially for small and mid-sized projects that have any type of community setting. Because small business owners and operators are besieged by requests for donations, many have a policy of not giving money. They are afraid that word will spread and then they will be obliged to write checks to everyone in the community who knocks on their door. Small businesses are much more likely to donates goods and services.

Two great things about small-business fundraising are that these businesses are so easy to approach, and so little paperwork is needed. The filmmaker can literally walk around the neighborhood and speak directly with business owners. Often the only paperwork that is needed is a simple one or two page write-up about the project, the crew, and what the business will receive in return for giving support.

A filmmaker I knew was working on a project that included student interns. Together they canvassed the neighborhood where the shoot would take place. Letters were sent in advance letting business owners know that the team would be contacting them. The letters included a list of the items needed by the film. After walking around and making their personal solicitations, the team was able to secure a number of goods and services that made a tremendous difference to the project, including free lunches for the crew, free photocopies of the scripts, and free use of cell phones during production. In return for support, the small businesses were mentioned in the end credits of the film and in all press releases. Other things that can be offered in thanks include guest appearance in the film as an extra; free and/or reduced-cost videocassette copies of the film; placement of the business logo on posters, tee shirts, and on film packaging; invitation to and prominent recognition at the local premiere and/or cast wrap party.

Students

I get many requests from undergraduate and graduate students asking how to raise support for their short film or thesis project. Unfortunately, I have mostly bad news for filmmakers in formal training programs who need money for their projects. Most foundations and government agencies have no interest at all in supporting the creation of student-made films. The exceptions might be those funders who have a vested interested in media education, but those are few and far between. Students generally will have to rely on scholarships and financial support available through their educational institutions.

If a student is serious about finding donations, then the best route would be to approach individuals – especially relatives. Throwing a fundraising houseparty or two might be appropriate. One creative solution that I heard involved a young filmmaker who sold shares in his future! The graduate student filmmaker made a promise to everyone who gave him funds to finish his thesis film: When he became a professional filmmaker and started making commercial films, they all would receive a small percentage of all his future profits.

Another common query I receive from students is if I know anyone who will just give them the equipment they need to make their films. The answer here, again, is "no." Funders shy away from giving money for the purchase of equipment, and manufacturers rarely will donate equipment. Entrepreneurial young filmmakers will, like their older cohorts, find ways to get access to the production and postproduction tools at either low or no cost, and then purchase the tools they need as their careers progress.

Morrie's Maxims

Before we say goodbye, I want to reiterate some points that have already been made, and bring up a few more. It is easy to feel overwhelmed by the enormous task of fundraising. And it is easy to lose sight of the bigger picture – how one film fits into the larger canvas of a whole career, and how fundraising is just one skill among many necessary to complete projects. So, just in case I have not been direct enough, let's revisit a few simple principles that help give context and focus to fundraising:

- **Personalize Everything.** Find ways to think like the funder, and provide the funder with the items that fulfill her needs. When possible, have communication come from someone already known to the funder.

- **Research Is Essential.** Research is just plain hard work, but must be done before approaching any funder.

- **Be Proactive.** Take control of every element in your environment that you can control, because even the smallest things are a reflection of your entire comportment.

- **Be Persistent.** Rejection is the norm in this business.

- **Write a Mission Statement.** Get clear about why filmmaking is absolutely essential to what you are trying to accomplish in the world, and be ready to articulate this mission to funders.

- **Learn How to Pitch.** Creating a brief and convincing pitch for each and every project is a baseline skill that must be part of the filmmaker's toolkit.

- **Network, Network, Network.** The best way to "curry serendipity" and increase the chances for unexpected but positive occurrences, is to get un-isolated and make as many contacts as possible.

- **Listen.** Learn the art of listening. Avoid monologue and invite dialogue as much as possible.

- **Say "Thank You."** Saying "thanks" costs almost nothing and reaps great rewards.

- **Stay in Touch.** Keep lines of communication open with past, present, and potential funders.

- **Market with Integrity.** Marketing is not a dirty word – it is an activity central to making a project and a filmmaker attractive to funders, and to helping a project ultimately find its audience. Find ways of marketing that are comfortable for you and your set of values.

- **Think Long-Term.** The journey of an independent filmmaker is a long one that takes stamina and a long-term vision. Be willing to suffer many short-term losses in return for long-term gains.

I hope this book has empowered the reader to embark on the process of fundraising with vigor, enthusiasm, and intelligence. Please feel free to send along stories of successes and failures, and any advice for additions or changes to future editions.

Now... go shake that money tree!

APPENDIX

SAMPLE GRANT

The sample grant that follows was graciously contributed by Paul Stekler. His proposal for the documentary *Settin' the Woods on Fire: The Life and Times of George Wallace* was funded by the National Endowment for the Humanities (NEH). The NEH has one of the more difficult grant forms, partly because the filmmaker must demonstrate expertise in the subject of the film, and must present a very detailed treatment. The proposal differs from many others in that it does not contain a section on distribution, and the budget must follow a standard NEH format that was not originally created for film. Otherwise, the proposal contains many lessons for beginning grant writers. I have taken the liberty of editing out sections of the full proposal in order to save space.

NEH APPLICATION COVER SHEET

OMB No. 3136-0086
Expires: 6/30/95

1. Individual applicant or project director

a. Name and mailing address

Name: Stekler, Paul J.

Address: Midnight Film

324 Broadway, 2nd Floor

New York, NY 10012

b. Form of address [Dr.]

c. Telephone number
212 - 925-1754 718 - 789-1345

d. Major field of applicant or project director: Political Science [PI]

e. Citizenship [X] U.S. [ ] Other

2. Type of applicant

a. [ ] by an individual b. [X] through an org./institution

c. Type: Public Media

d. Status: Private Non-Profit

3. Type of application

a. [X] New b. [ ] Supplement

4. Program to which application is being made

Humanities Projects in Media

5. Requested grant period

From: November 1995 to: March 1997

6. Project funding

a. Outright funds $ 948,022

b. Federal match $ ___

c. Total from NEH $ 948,022

d. Cost sharing $ ___

e. Total project costs $ 948,022

7. Field of project [A3]

8. Descriptive title of project
SETTIN' THE WOODS ON FIRE: THE LIFE AND TIMES OF GEORGE WALLACE

9. Description of project (do not exceed space provided) This application is for the Production Phase of a two hour historical documentary entitled SETTIN' THE WOODS ON FIRE: THE LIFE AND TIMES OF GEORGE WALLACE. The project has already received Scripting funding from the NEH. The film will explore the political life of the man who became the best known opponent of civil rights in America, from his rural Alabama boyhood, through his early career as a racially moderate populist, and into his reinvention of himself as the champion of alienated voters, known variously as "the silent majority" and the "white backlash." Culminating in his campaigns for the presidency, where some say he changed the national political agenda, the story of Wallace's political career will be interwoven with the history of the civil rights movement and the fracturing of American politics in the 1960s and 70s. The film is the project of filmmaker Paul Stekler, whose previous films include *Eyes on the Prize* and *Last Stand at Little Bighorn*, in addition to *Louisiana Boys: Raised on Politics* and other films about politics in the South. The film is intended for a national public television audience.

10. Will this proposal be submitted to another government agency or private source? If yes, indicate where and when: Previous research and scripting outlay by the NEH, the PBS, and the state humanities councils of ALA, GBH, LA, MISS, NC, SC, TENN, and VIR.

11. Institutional data

a. Institution or organization
Filmmakers Collaborative

Boston MA

b. Employer Identification number 22-2773829

c. Name of authorizing official
Zimbergan, John
Title Secretary-Treasurer

d. Name and mailing address of institutional grant administrator
Zuckerman, John
Filmmakers' Collaborative
63 Endicott St., Room 503
Boston, MA 02113

Telephone 617 - 367-6812 Form of address [Mr.]

12. Certification
By signing and submitting this application, the individual or the authorizing official of the applicant institution (block 11a) is providing the applicable certifications regarding the nondiscrimination statutes and implementing regulations, federal debt status, debarment and suspension, a drug-free workplace, and lobbying activities, as set forth in the appropriate regulations and guidelines.

Signature   Date

For NEH use only

COVER SHEET CONTINUATION

A) The FILMMAKERS' COLLABORATIVE was founded in 1987 by seven independent film and video makers committed to producing socially relevant work. Their intention was to form an organization which would provide mutual support and fiscal sponsorship for work considered too risky to produce on a for-profit basis. Recent documentary projects that have received grant support through the organization include: Paul Stekler's NEH-supported LAST STAND AT LITTLE BIGHORN, which aired on PBS's series THE AMERICAN EXPERIENCE; Laurie Kahn-Levin's NEH-supported MIDWIFE'S TALE; Carl Nagin, Carma Hilton and Richard Gordon's NEH-supported CHANG TA CHIEN FILM PROJECT; Michal Goldman's NEH-supported film on Umm Kulthum; and Michal Aviad's ACTING OUR AGE, about cultural myths concerning women and aging, which aired on PBS's P.O.V. series.

B) SETTIN THE WOODS ON FIRE: THE LIFE AND TIMES OF GEORGE WALLACE is the story of the life of an American politician who was seen as America's best known opponent of civil rights in the 1960s, who ran for president three times and who held the reins of power in Alabama's government for nearly two decades – and whose influence on today's national political dialogue is still seen by many historians. His is a story interwoven with the history of the civil rights movement in the South, the rise of white backlash, and the fracturing of American politics in the late 1960s and 70s.

Among the many themes this film will explore, involving American political history from the 1940s onward, are: the realignment of American politics and party balance in the 1960s and 70s; the rise of the "alienated" voter and the "social issue" during that same period; the origins and consequences of America's civil rights movement; the enduring nature and identity of the South as a product of white Southern history; and the role and responsibilities of elected leaders – and of the electorate – in a representative democracy.

C) SETTIN THE WOODS ON FIRE: THE LIFE AND TIMES OF GEORGE WALLACE will be a 2 hour documentary shot on film and edited on an Avid. The film will be comprised of historical documentary film footage and photographs as well as original interviews and on-location shooting in Alabama. The film, produced by a production team with numerous national public television credits, is aimed at a national PBS audience. It will also be distributed to schools, libraries, and individuals on video.

D) KEY PERSONNEL: Paul Stekler, Project Director/ Producer. Steve Fayer, Writer. Dan McCabe, Editor.

CONSULTANTS: Dan Carter, Emory University, Chief Advisor. Jack Bass, University of Mississippi. Merle Black, Emory University. Alan Brinkley, Columbia University. David Garrow, College of William and Mary. Virginia Van der Veer Hamilton, University of Alabama at Birmingham. Lawrence Hanks, University of Indiana. Gary Orren, Harvard University. Linda Reed, University of Houston. John Shelton Reed, University of North Carolina. J. Mills Thornton, University of Michigan.

SUPPORTING MATERIAL:

Videotapes
EYES ON THE PRIZE - "The Promised Land 1967-68", co-produced by Paul Stekler (1990)
LOUISIANA BOYS - RAISED ON POLITICS, co-produced by Paul Stekler (1991)
LAST STAND AT LITTLE BIGHORN, produced by Paul Stekler (1992)

SETTIN' THE WOODS ON FIRE:
THE LIFE AND TIMES OF GEORGE WALLACE

Introduction: Goals and Objectives

"You can tell your grandchildren that there was once a whirlwind that blew through this country. Blew all through this land. And that whirlwind was George Wallace. You can tell your grandchildren that."

— George Wallace
after a political rally in Mobile,
Alabama, 1982, told to Paul Stekler

"He (was) the complete democratic demagogue, the political creature carried to the ultimate — fascinating as are all pure specimens of a kind... In a sense, Wallace is common to us all. That, finally, is his darkest portent. There is something primordially exciting and enthralling about him, and there still seems to be just enough of the wolf pack in most of us to be stirred by it and to answer to it. As long as we are creatures hung halfway between the cave and the stars, figures like Wallace can be said to pose the great dark original threat."

— Marshall Frady
Wallace

George Wallace. In the 1960s and 70s, he symbolized resistance to civil rights in this country. He was the man who stood in the schoolhouse door, barring black students from the University of Alabama. He was the man who looked out at America and said "segregation now, segregation tomorrow, and segregation forever." The images remain of huge crowds laughing, shouting, jeering, exhilarated by the furious energy of Wallace's snarling attacks against people he called hippies, civil rights agitators, welfare recipients, beatniks, anti-war protesters, communists, and street thugs who had "turned to rape and murder 'cause they didn't get enough broccoli when they were little boys."

Wallace was one of many Southern politicians to rise to power on the issue of race — but he alone rose to real national political prominence, the flashpoint of a national backlash against the civil rights movement. In the words of one biographer, Wallace seemingly single-handedly "alerted the national custodians to a massive, unsuspected, unanswered constituency, a great submerged continent of discontent." Dubbed "white backlash" and the "silent majority," they were alienated and angry. Wallace's entrance as their champion could not have been timed better. In the midst of the collapse of the Johnson presidency and the Democratic New Deal coalition — and in the aftermath of the assassinations of Martin Luther King and Robert Kennedy, the urban riots and the breakdown of politics as people had known it — he came to symbolize a kind of national disorder, what one writer described in 1968 as "the sense of a certain berserkness in the national life."

Demagogue, spokesman, garish caricature. Governor, national figure, third-party candidate for President. A man who many thought might win enough electoral votes to throw a presidential election into the United States Congress — and then hold the office hostage to his position on race. A tireless campaigner shot down by a would-be assassin on the eve of his greatest national victories. George Wallace.

Settin' the Woods on Fire: The Life and Times of George Wallace, a two-hour historical television documentary, will be both a film biography, fitting into the NEH's special initiative on "American Lives", and an examination of the forces let loose in America during a time of great and sometimes violent change. Virtually all previous documentary film work dealing with this period of American history explores this story from the perspective of the civil rights movement. *Settin' the Woods on Fire* will add to the story told by series like the much-honored *Eyes on the Prize* (two episodes of which were co-produced by *Wallace* project director Paul Stekler) adjusting the frame through which this history is told in order to examine the people and the forces opposed to change. As historian Alan Brinkley, a project advisor, has noted, "despite an enormous array of scholarship and films of the civil rights movement, virtually nothing examines the opposition. Wallace was the most visible and important example of the white opposition movement and deserves attention." And as Linda Reed, the Director of African-American Studies at the University of Houston and another project advisor, adds, "If you look at the full picture of the civil rights struggle, people have to understand the opposition in order to understand the victory."

Civil rights activists in the early 1960s clearly won the moral high ground, risking their lives to force the enactment of national legislation. As David Garrow powerfully illustrates in his book *Protest at Selma*, the movement used the public reaction outside of the South, in response to the actions of Southern officials like Wallace and to televised acts of violence against civil rights activists, to force legislative action. But not everyone watching Wallace, "standing in the schoolhouse door" or speaking against what he claimed were the excesses of federal power, disagreed with him. As Andrew Young, Martin Luther King's chief aide at the Southern Christian Leadership Conference, has since stated, "Wallace had been a great help to us in his opposition in Alabama," his uncompromising stands drawing federal action and national public distaste. "But when he began to attract followers in Michigan, in Wisconsin, places that we thought were liberal states, it was clearly a threat."

Today, many historians argue that the resistance championed by George Wallace ultimately had a profound impact on the nation's politics and policies in the following decades. Wallace was often explicitly racist in his rhetoric, especially in the early 1960s, touting the threat of racial "mongrelization" and warning of hundreds of thousands of "nigger votes." Yet his broader message of running against the bureaucrats in

Washington, against "big government," can be clearly linked to the appeals of every President since the 1960s. In 1986, when *Eyes on the Prize* producer Callie Crossley asked Wallace to defend his record in office, especially his time in the national limelight opposing civil rights, he replied:

> "I spoke vehemently against the federal government, not against people. I talked about the government of the United States and the Supreme Court. I never expressed this in any language that would upset anyone about a person's race. I talked about the Supreme Court's usurpation of power. I talked about big central government. Isn't that what everybody talks about now?"

Many historians are asking the same question. Jack Bass, author of six books about Southern politics and history, wrote in 1988:

> "Liberals. Coddled criminals. Welfare cheats. Federal bureaucrats. In the 1960s, George Wallace denounced them all. To many people in that era of rapid social change, his message seemed like the retrograde rantings of a political throwback. But now that his issues are the popular orthodoxy of the day, historians are taking a closer look at the man who started it all."

Settin' the Woods on Fire: The Life and Times of George Wallace will be the first in-depth documentary look at this history from within the context of Wallace's life, his career in politics, and the people who supported him.

The political transformations that George Wallace made during his life were dramatic. In the late 1940s and early 50s, Wallace, a populist disciple of the legendary "Big Jim" Folsom, was known as one of the most liberal members of the Alabama state legislature, a "do-gooder" who asked the governor to make him a trustee at Tuskegee Institute, the state's black university. But in the aftermath of a crushing loss to an extreme segregationist in Wallace's first campaign for governor, and amid the Southern anti-civil rights hysteria that followed the Supreme Court's Brown v. Board of Education ruling, Wallace vowed never to be "out-niggered" again. Making race the core of his message, he won the governorship in the early 1960s and helped inflame a series of civil rights confrontations — always knowing the buttons he was pushing. In a private aside to a newspaper publisher who wanted to know how he felt about abandoning the idealism of his political youth, Wallace said: "I started off talking about schools and highways and prisons and taxes — and I couldn't make them listen. Then I began talking about niggers — and they stomped the floor."

As white backlash grew in the midst of summers of urban violence and growing racial polarization, Wallace leapt onto the national political stage — running for President in 1964, 1968, and 1972. Adjusting his rhetoric for his larger audience, he made his issues "law and order," opposition to big government, and anti-busing. Yet in the aftermath of his shooting, paralyzed, in constant pain, and now aware of a growing active black electorate in Alabama in the 1970s and 80s, Wallace was again transformed. He became the self-proclaimed "governor of all Alabamians," an ally of state social and educational programs, dependent on the black vote to stay in office. And he begged forgiveness from his former opponents, saying that he had been wrong.

Settin' the Woods on Fire: The Life and Times of George Wallace will be produced and directed by filmmaker Paul Stekler. Dr. Stekler, whose PhD dissertation focused on politics in the post-civil rights American South, has made six films on American politics and history, all of which have been nationally broadcast on public television. In the last five years, his films have included two episodes of the acclaimed *Eyes on the Prize II* series (winner of the Organization of American Historian's Erik Barnouw Award, a Peabody Award, and the duPont-Columbia Award), *Louisiana Boys: Raised on Politics* (a duPont-Columbia award-winning film about Louisiana political culture that aired nationally on public television's P.O.V. series), *Last Stand at Little Bighorn* (co-written with Native-American novelist James Welch), an NEH supported film reexamining the Battle of the Little Bighorn that attracted over six million viewers for its initial PBS airing on THE AMERICAN EXPERIENCE and won an Emmy Award, and *Vote for Me: Politics in America*, a series about American political culture that will be the centerpiece of PBS's election year programming in 1996. Previously, Stekler taught Southern politics at Tulane University in New Orleans, where he made two award-winning independent documentaries about African-American politics in the South.

The distinguished production team for this film will include Emmy Award-winning writer Steve Fayer (series writer for *Eyes on the Prize*, *Eyes on the Prize II*, and for the NEH-supported series *The Great Depression series*; co-writer for *Malcolm X: Make it Plain*); editor Dan McCabe (editor on the *Nixon* series, *Columbus and the Age of Discovery*, and the *Eisenhower* series); and chief advisor Dan Carter, the Andrew W. Mellon Professor in the Humanities at Emory University and Bancroft Award winning historian (*Scottsboro: A Tragedy of the American South*), whose major new biography of George Wallace, *The Politics of Rage: George Wallace and His America*, will be published by Simon & Schuster later this year.

Settin' the Woods on Fire: The Life and Times of George Wallace will be a compelling, emotional, and dramatic blend of archival film, photographs, and interviews with major political figures and plain folk, white and black, whose lives and experiences were caught up in both the life of George Wallace and the tides of history in which he moved. This material will be intercut with present-day cinematography of the evocative landscapes and remaining older architecture of the American South, and enhanced by commentary from writers and scholars familiar with the South and with Wallace. By the end of *Settin' the Woods on Fire*, the viewing audience will better understand the forces of history that pushed Wallace to the forefront of national politics, better understand the perspectives of the people who either supported or opposed him — and better understand the political legacy that outlived his public career.

Humanities Themes

> "We don't stop and figure, we don't think about history
> or theories or none of that. We just go ahead. Hell,
> history can take care of itself."

> — George Wallace, 1966

The Life and Times of George Wallace will go beyond straight biography to use the life and political career of George Wallace to examine a number of broader humanities issues involving questions of representation in a democratic society and the causes and consequences of political change in our country. The humanities themes threading through this film include:

- The realignment of American politics and party balance in the 1960s and 70s;
- The rise of the "alienated" voter and the "social issue" during that same period;
- The origins and consequences of America's civil rights movement;
- The enduring nature and identity of the American South;
- The role and responsibilities of elected leaders in a representative democracy:
- The role of responsibilities of the electorate — do we get the leaders we deserve?

Wallace's life and the events surrounding it make for an extremely dramatic and compelling story. The rise of the civil rights movement in the South and the concurrent rise of massive Southern white resistance in the 1950s and 60s are integral to understanding this history.

Birmingham and Selma, freedom marchers and police dogs, church bombings and murders of civil rights volunteers, Martin Luther King writing his "Letter from a Birmingham Jail" and George Wallace "standing in the schoolhouse door" — these are images that are seared onto our collective memories of those times. And for the generation of Americans who have grown up since these events, this film project is an opportunity to experience the terrible and the heartening lessons these moments contained.

This story also is interwoven with some of the most dramatic electoral politics that this country has ever seen. Wallace's third-party candidacy, that attracted over ten million voters, played itself out in the melodrama of 1968 as the nation seemed to totter on the edge of societal breakdown, amidst assassinations and protest and civil disorder. The major characters in this drama are a mix of political giants and fascinating supporting players: the Kennedys, Lyndon Johnson and Richard Nixon; Martin Luther King and the grassroots movement people who risked their lives in the struggle for civil rights; and the people of Alabama whose lives were intertwined with Wallace's from the start of his career in politics until its end. Among them were: "Big" Jim Folsom, the six foot eight populist, Wallace's first political mentor whose flawed career was described by one observer as doomed by "too much whiskey, too many women, too few honest friends"; Judge Frank M. Johnson, one of Wallace's closest friends at law school, whose rulings in favor of civil rights in Alabama made him the brunt of Wallace's virulent attacks on court ordered desegregation; Wallace's first wife Lurleen, the shy, long neglected wife, suffering from ovarian cancer, who was pushed into running for governor as her husband's surrogate — and won; and a host of others. And finally, too, there is the shooting of candidate Wallace, on the eve of his greatest national victories in 1972.

As this film uses the life of George Wallace to explore the dynamics of American politics and to pose questions about our representative democracy, it will touch on many humanities fields: history, politics, literature, and popular culture (particularly the image of the South in the American imagination) among them.

Wallace is seen by many contemporary political analysts and modern historians as a pivotal figure in the collapse of the Democratic Party's New Deal national majority coalition. He is also seen as an important transitional figure in articulating the demands (and fears) of the masses of "backlash" or "alienated" voters, and mobilizing them "to send Washington a message." Their votes eventually became part of a new national "conservative" majority that dominated presidential races for the next two decades. Dan Carter, the project's chief academic advisor, in his letter of support in this application, flatly states:

> "I don't think we can make any sense of American politics in the 1960s and 1970s (indeed in the decade that followed) without understanding the critical role George Wallace played in transforming those politics."

There are many questions to be explored. How does examining Wallace help us understand the dynamic forces that changed the partisan balance and the nature of political debate in the United States during this period? And how does Wallace help us to understand the growing voter alienation and reaction in the country at that time? Who made up the ranks of the "white backlash" and what were their feelings and thoughts? And, finally, what is the legacy today of those political changes of which Wallace and his supporters were a part?

In his day, Wallace became much more than a mere Dixie demagogue — but he never lost his "Southern" identity in the mind of the American public. How does focusing on Wallace, the best known exponent of white Southern resistance to the civil rights movement in his time, help us to understand the white South? And if we use the white South as "context," how does an understanding of both Southern history and the enduring Southern identity help us to understand Wallace, his political style and his political appeal?

Wallace's career in politics is inseparable from the history of the civil rights movement in the South; so many of the dramatic confrontations of that time took place in Alabama during Wallace's years in power.

What role did he play in that history? How did the movement use the public's perceptions of officials like Wallace, especially those images captured by television, to further their goals — and how did Wallace use that same medium to make himself a national figure?

Finally, what is the role and responsibility of elected representatives in a democratic society? Should one expect elected officials "to lead" the people they represent, or to simply follow the wishes of their constituents? In the South of the late 1950s and 60s, the public choices available to elected white officials who desired reelection seemed narrow. But, in reality, there were a range of possible responses. Did Wallace knowingly manipulate the tensions of the times, making them more confrontational and more violent, in order to further his political career? Are comparisons between Wallace's political career and the career of people like Judge Frank Johnson useful in evaluating the possibilities and limits of representative democracy during periods of societal upheaval?

Civil Rights, White Reaction, and National Political Realignment

National political realignment in the 1960s and afterwards can be linked to both the civil rights movement in the South and the subsequent "backlash" reaction (reaction that in the South was against civil rights; and outside of the South was in response to a myriad of issues, of which black empowerment was but one facet). The Democratic New Deal coalition of Southern whites, Northern blacks, and urban ethnic whites comprised a majority of the American electorate after the 1930s, but it was also a very fragile coalition. Northern urban blacks and white ethnics supported similar liberal policy initiatives advocated by the Democratic Party, but they co-existed in American cities where whites held political power and blacks did not threaten that power. White Southern allegiance to the national Democratic Party was partially based on the post-Reconstruction establishment of a one-party Democratic South, where the Democratic Party in the South was legally the party of "whites only." When the system of white supremacy in the South was challenged and the alignment of power in American cities began to change, the New Deal coalition moved towards an inevitable collapse.

Nicholas Lemann, in his book *The Promised Land*, ties all of this to the great black migration out of the South in the twentieth century, a product of the mechanization of agriculture and the mass desire to escape the social, economic, and political oppression of the region. This migration created a much greater awareness of African-American culture and an increasingly large black population living up north where blacks could vote. This, in turn, increased their influence within the national Democratic Party. The Party's decision to allow a stronger civil rights plank to pass at its 1948 national convention (precipitating a Southern walkout and Strom Thurmond's Dixiecrat presidential candidacy) was the first indication of this growing black voting strength. The Party's subsequent move towards advocacy of national civil rights legislation, including federal intervention in the South, in the later 1950s and 60s, was an outgrowth of this. But, as Lemann writes, there was significant reaction to these developments:

> "It hardly created a harmonious, racially synthesized country. The government's response to the migration provided the (modern) conservative movement with many of its issues. The idea that government programs don't work, and can't work, comes out of the Great Society, and particularly the war on poverty; all through his political career, one of Ronald Reagan's favorite sayings was, 'In the 1960s we fought a war on poverty, and poverty won.' So does the idea that most middle-class people are paying too much federal income tax to support harebrained social betterment schemes, which was central to Reagan's (and therefore also George Bush's) rise to the presidency. In intellectual life, the neo-conservative movement, whose influence on Republican policy-making has been enormous, was founded by former liberals who lost faith in large part over the issue of race in the North."

What was George Wallace's role in this? Clearly, he had nothing to do with setting the larger forces — mass migration, national Democratic Party policy in the 1940s and 50s — in motion. But once demographic changes, Supreme Court rulings, and white resistance to the earliest stirrings of a Southern civil rights movement set this dynamic in motion, Wallace became a pivotal player in the political transformations that followed. In the aftermath of Wallace's 1968 third-party candidacy against the Republican victor Richard Nixon and the Democratic nominee, Vice-President Hubert Humphrey, author Kevin Phillips was already forecasting that the ten million votes cast for Wallace were destined to become part of a new national majority. In his widely read book *The Emerging Republican Majority*, Phillips placed Wallace in the larger context of the demise of the Democratic Party in the South:

> "The Dixiecrat party (in 1948) served many conservatives as a way station between a no longer appealing Democratic Party and the increasingly Southern-concerned GOP. History will doubtless label George Wallace's party a similar way-station for another element of Southern voters. Most of the poor whites whom Wallace broke loose from the Democrats have lined up against newly enfranchised Negroes just as they did in the somewhat comparable Reconstruction Era of a century ago. Now that the national Democratic Party is becoming the Negro party throughout most of the South, the alienation of white Wallace voters is likely to persist... (But) the Wallace movement cannot maintain an adequate political base and is bound to serve, like past American third parties, as a way station for groups abandoning one party for another — towards the GOP."

With this in mind, Harry Dent, an aide of Strom Thurmond and the architect of Nixon's successful "Southern strategy," urged President Nixon in a 1969 White House memo to follow Phillips' plan and court Wallace's supporters — though, he hastened to add, the Republicans should "disavow it publicly."

Yet even as Phillips treated Wallace's third party campaign as a temporary resting spot for future Republican voters, he noted Wallace's "populist" ability to mobilize alienated working-class white voters. In part, this owed to Wallace's ability to get white working-class voters to see something of themselves in him. After all, Wallace was an ex-Golden Gloves fighter, a former truck driver who had married a dime store clerk. But some analysts believed that this appeal went beyond Wallace's working-class style, noting that many of Wallace's northern working-class white ethnic following had also supported Bobby Kennedy before his assassination.

Was Wallace's extraordinary appeal based solely on his more extreme racial stances? Historian Alan Brinkley, thinking about this link between Wallace and his supporters, asks: "to what degree was race an autonomous category and to what degree was race simply an invented category to disguise concerns about other things like class." The rise of what was termed "the social issue" — the call for "law and order" in the face of growing crime, the condemnation of social and cultural permissiveness, the opposition to affirmative action and school busing — and its use as a political battle cry against big government and the federal bureaucracy, while partially rooted in race, covered much broader ground. And it was into this fertile political soil that George Wallace took his national campaigns.

In the 1960s, Wallace sensed and then exploited the changes that America came to know by many names: white backlash, the silent majority, the alienated voters. As Dan Carter has written: "Clearly something dramatic was happening in American politics. George Wallace had touched the chords of angry discontent across the nation. And for the better part of the next decade, Wallace would rise to be the impresario of the politics of anger."

By the mid-1960s, the civil rights movement had used its local campaigns in places like Birmingham and Selma, to establish the issue of race in terms of right versus wrong, civil rights and freedom versus a history of racial oppression. Night after night, this Southern drama was played out on television sets nationwide. Voters listed civil rights as the most important issue facing the country. Historic civil rights legislation was enacted and a barrage of Great Society programs was launched. As Nicholas Lemann writes:

> "The civil rights movement in the South had brilliantly practiced media politics, and its historic victories were immensely aided by the presence of easily identifiable heroes (like Dr. King) and villains (like George Wallace)."

But any semblance of a national consensus on race exploded as urban violence tore through the nation's cities. The riots, and white reaction against growing militancy in black communities (and growing black challenges for urban political power), accelerated the conservative reaction that became known as "white backlash."

Wallace, the "villain" in the morality play of civil rights in the South, seized the moment to make his entrance onto the national political stage. He transcended the explicitly racist rhetoric of the old South, adapting it to Northern sensibilities by talking in code. Battle cries for "states' rights," "constitutionalism," and "the Southern way of life," became "law and order," "individual property rights," and a defense of the people against the tyranny of "big government." When Wallace opposed the Civil Rights Act of 1964, for example, he claimed that it was not because he was against the rights of blacks. He said he was against:

> "an infringement upon the property rights system... I don't believe there is a backlash in this country because of color. I think that's a journalistic expression. I think it was coined by the news media. I think there's a backlash against the theoreticians and the bureaucrats in national government. There isn't a backlash among the mass of American people against anybody because of color. There's a backlash against big government in this country."

Wallace named his targets: "intellectual morons who don't know how to park a bicycle straight," "pointy-headed professors," the national press ("who are going to get some of those liberal smiles knocked off their faces"), "Federal judges playing God," and bureaucrats, most of whom "have beards."

His audience understood his code. As Lewis Chester, Godfrey Hodgson, and Bruce Page, in their book *An American Melodrama: The Presidential Campaign of 1968*, write:

> "George Wallace was able to march north because he had found a set of rhetorical keys which would open many political boxes in America in 1968. He knew how to denounce what was happening in such terms that those for whom the most important problem was the Negro Revolution believed he was merely spelling n-i-g-g-e-r in a new way, while millions of others who were not obsessed with race nevertheless felt he cared about the issues that troubled them."

Thus, Wallace offered an alternative diagnosis for America's ills. Where the problem had once been defined, by many, as "white racism," in his rhetoric it became "big government" and bureaucratic interference. According to Thomas and Mary Edsall, the authors of *Chain Reaction: The Impact of Race, Rights, and Taxes on American Politics*, Wallace's main impact on American politics was to build a constituency based on this re-framing of the American problem. The cost of distributing economic and citizenship rights more equitably to blacks and to other minorities, from this perspective, "fell primarily on working and lower-middle class whites who frequently competed with blacks for jobs and status, who lived in neighborhoods adjoining black ghettos, and whose children attended schools most likely to fall under busing orders." The resentment of these white, working-class voters, the Edsalls write, "was increasingly amplified and channeled... not just toward blacks, but toward Wallace's original target: the affluent, largely white universe of liberal "experts" who were pressing the legal claims of blacks and other minorities — experts often sheltered, in their private lives, and largely immune to the costs of implementing minority claims."

The election of 1968, where fifty six percent of the voters rejected a liberal Democratic ticket (Richard Nixon winning with forty three percent; Wallace taking thirteen percent), seemed to validate a new "Southern strategy" of courting disaffected white Democrats. As subsequent national elections seemed to build a solid national Republican presidential majority, "race" began to be seen as a losing issue for national Democrats. Both the Edsalls and E. J. Dionne, in his book *Why Americans Hate Politics*, point out that issues involving race increasingly became relegated to either largely symbolic gestures or a persistent rehashing of old debates over the merits or failures of the Great Society. Thus, few meaningful policy alternatives were offered to the electorate, in the 1970s or 80s, as the day-to-day lives of the urban poor grew worse, urban economies collapsed, and the racial cleavages in the country grew wider.

David Garrow, the noted biographer of Martin Luther King and historian of the civil rights movement, asks in retrospect: "Did Wallace lose the civil rights battle, but win the rhetorical battle for the national political agenda?" Every American president since the 1960s has incorporated Wallace's anti-Washington, anti-Big Government "outsider" rhetoric in order to win office. Political scientist Gary Orren points out that Wallace helped shift the debate in the country to the right in the 1960s and 70s, likening his influence on Richard Nixon to that of Huey Long on Franklin Delano Roosevelt. The threat of a Long third-party candidacy in 1936, that would drain votes from FDR, created the political motivation for the President's heralded "turn to the left" (a series of ambitious New Deal policies that Brinkley notes in his book *Voices of Protest*). Three decades later, Richard Nixon's domestic agenda turned to the right in response to the popularity of Wallace's more conservative appeals to supporters. As Dan Carter writes:

"For nearly ten years George Wallace helped to shape the texture of American rhetoric. There was never any likelihood that he would be elected president of the United States; he was too raw, too crude, too Southern. But he had been one of the great transitional figures in American politics. Poltergeist, weathervane: Wallace served both roles in the America of the 1960s and 1970s as he developed a respectable rhetoric to cloak the cruder vocabulary of traditional racism and to give shape and focus to that whole range of social issues from abortion to banned Bible reading to crime in the streets — the social issues that would come to dominate the rhetoric of American politics."

In his letter of support in this application, project advisor Gary Orren adds:

"George Wallace not only dominated national politics from 1964 until 1972 when he was shot, but he was the critical catalyst for electoral trends during the Nixon, Carter, and Reagan years. National politicians either rode the waves which Wallace identified, stirred up, and tried to ride himself or they struggled against those waves. To a large extent — on domestic issues — Wallace set the terms of the national political agenda and dialogue."

Those issues and that alienated electorate remain important today. Understanding Wallace's appeal, and Wallace's supporters, likewise, remains relevant.

Wallace and the White South

"The South was created by the need to protect a peculiar institution (slavery) from the threats originating outside the region. Consequently, the Southern identity has been linked from the first to a siege mentality. (White Southerners see themselves) defending their region against attack from outside forces: abolitionists, the Union Army, carpetbaggers, Wall Street and Pittsburgh, civil rights agitators, the Federal Government, feminism, socialism, trade unionism, Darwinism, communism, atheism, daylight savings time, and other by-products of modernity."

— Sheldon Hackney
Southern Violence

"What was important to (Wallace) was the feelings of people, mainly working class rural whites. He was an ethnic leader. (And) through George Wallace, it was them out-smarting that fast talking, smart ass Yankee reporter from CBS. The South is winning. I am winning. I am finally having my day."

— Bill Ayers, publisher
Anniston Star
Anniston, Alabama

Even in today's mass media culture, the American South remains distinct. Where would American literature and movies be without Southern gentlemen and belles, redneck villains and comic backwoods hillbillies, Southern sheriffs, Delta blues musicians, rural preachers, and flowery politicians in long white suits? The Southern demagogue, part Senator Claghorn and part Huey Long, competes with only the Irish city

boss (part *Last Hurrah*, part Richard Daley), as the most distinctive political character in American popular culture as well. This, in part, is due
to the connotations that the Southern identity has had in the popular
American imagination.

The preconceived "image" of Southern social types is one that consis-
tently has confronted Southerners in their contact with their fellow
Americans. George Wallace, remembering his early army days in basic
training, outside of Denver, tells a story that illustrates this:

> "(There) was a bunch of girls working at the PX, and
> me and my buddy (from Mississippi) went in and asked
> 'em for a can of snuff. They asked us what our fathers
> did and I told 'em my daddy was in the penitentiary for
> makin' whiskey. They smiled and got all giggly —
> those gals had found 'em some real live hillbillies. I
> asked 'em, "How'd you like to go sparkin'?" They
> agreed to go to a motion picture — a hundred thou-
> sand soldiers out there they wouldn't give a date to.
> They were so gullible."

Sociologist John Shelton Reed, citing this story, says that these women,
filtering Wallace and his friend through their prior perceptions of
Southerners, had "George Wallace pegged." And while enjoying his
immediate advantage, Wallace himself acknowledged the reality that
people "thought you were just ignorant 'cause you came from the
South." It is an image that American popular culture, especially movies
and television, has helped nurture: one that was reinforced in the 1960s
and 70s by *The Beverly Hillbillies, The Dukes of Hazzard* and Burt
Reynolds' *Smokey and the Bandit* films. Citing an earlier generation of
war movies, Texas columnist Molly Ivons remembers:

> "You take all those old movies around the World War II
> era. I don't know how many zillions there were, but the
> classic World War II movie consists of an all-American,
> clean cut hero who's usually from somewhere in the

middle West, usually a farm kid from Kansas who's blonde. And he's always got one wise-cracking buddy from New York. And then there's always some just dumb, slow-talking Southerner who's the butt of all the jokes in the military movie. And that's a stock character in the military movie, and it really has reinforced the prejudice against a Southern accent."

It is important to remember that George Wallace was perceived by much of the rest of the nation to personify the white South in the 1960s. And Wallace, as a politician, was clearly a product of the South.

The post-Reconstruction South became a solid one-party Democratic region, established as such to institutionalize white rule. The Democratic Party in Southern states was legally restricted to whites (even as most Southern blacks were barred from registering to vote) and only Democrats won general elections. All successful candidates thus shared the same party label in the only election that mattered, the Democratic primary. The result noted by V. O. Key in his 1949 classic study *Southern Politics* were elections that produced "a chaotic factional politics." Voters facing ballots with long lists of candidates who were all Democrats, tended to vote for candidates that they had seen or met, knew or had heard of, usually from their part of the state. Key called it "friends and neighbors voting."

It was in the interest of candidates for statewide office, who in the days before television were not easily "known" by a bulk of the white electorate, to then figure out a way, as Merle and Earl Black note in *Politics and Society in the South*, to "stand out in a crowd." It was no coincidence that the South became dominated by demagoguery. Sensational accusations and no holds barred attacks against blacks and Yankees marked the careers of the "Cotton Ed" Smiths, "Pitchfork" Ben Tillmans, Theo Bilbos, and their like. As the Blacks write:

"The common touch was indispensable. Colorful phrases, memorable anecdotes with well-conceived

> punch lines, an ability to defend one's honesty and integrity at the drop of an accusation or attack an opponent's character, intelligence, ancestry, and morals should the occasion demand it — such attributes were all part of the paraphernalia necessary to survive in the mass political culture of the rural and small-town South."

Countrified verbal slugging came naturally to most ambitious young politicians. Without it, they would have trouble winning office. Wallace was successful at it — and he was able to "study at the knee" of one of the best, "Big Jim" Folsom, "the little man's big friend."

Folsom was one of the most liberal politicians ever produced by the South. Twice the governor of Alabama, he stood for governmental protection of the poor, equal opportunity, and full access to the ballot, long before the voting rights legislation of the 1960s. Back in the late 40s, he was denouncing the Ku Klux Klan for "spreading their filth, their lies, their old and ancient hatreds... trying to boil up hatred by the poor white people against Negroes... trying to keep poor whites from progressing by keeping the Negro in shackles."

Folsom was one of a number of authentic champions of the common man — Senators Lister Hill, John Sparkman, and Hugo Black and Congressman Carl Elliott, among others — who sprang up from the roots of Alabama populism. In Congress, they provided leadership for major programs in education, public health, and housing. Their political battles in Alabama were the continuation of a century of warfare between poor white farmers and their conservative foes, the large planters of the Black Belt and their "Big Mule" business allies. George Wallace's advocacy of state-funded programs as a young state legislator in the 1940s echoed the appeals of the populist Farmer's Alliance in the 1890s, led by Reuben Kolb, who called for state control of banks and railroads and regulation of the big planters' control of sharecroppers. After all, George Wallace was a man that college friends described as "a real Franklin Delano Roosevelt socialist."

In the politics of the deep South, though, there was another side of "populist" politics and it inevitably revolved around the condition of blacks — mostly in guaranteeing their continued oppression and disenfranchisement. Again and again, Southern populists (many of whom were "populist" in rhetoric only) used racism against blacks to unify their white constituents, and to guarantee their continued electoral support. As Virginia Van der Veer Hamilton, the biographer of Lister Hill, notes:

> "Hill voted against everything, from anti-lynching laws to all the major civil rights bills in order to stay in office. And justified his action by saying, 'what would you have me do, get defeated, and then no one would pass health legislation?'"

This was the other face of Alabama populism to which Wallace turned in his later career.

Mills Thornton, the historian of both 19th and 20th century Alabama, sees Wallace representing the white South's feelings of both its "underdog status" — in relation to the rest of the country that they believed was looking down on them — and its "overdog" status, in the desire to maintain white supremacy in the region. Wallace, as a defender of a "lost cause," struck an emotional chord in many Southerners. Thornton notes:

> "His importance as a figure in Southern history, in a sense, is as a symbol of the white South as it makes the final and painful transition away from a set of institutions and attitudes that had been ingrained in the region since the turn of the century. Wallace's reward for having led the South to defeat is that he emerges as the great figure of Alabama politics and is rewarded with five terms as governor — if you count his wife's single term."

Many of Wallace's Southern supporters personally identified with him as he led their fight. As a former aide of Wallace once noted:

> "All those little farmhouses stuck way out in the woods, they all had a TV set, you know. When those folks saw Wallace on there standin' up to those big-city slick-hair boys, that wasn't just him talkin'. That was them on there."

Even Southerners less enamored of the Alabama governor found Wallace hard to escape. John Shelton Reed, as a young graduate student from a Tennessee mountain Republican family, recalls one incident during his years up North:

> "I still remember sitting in my dissertation advisor's living room in Westport, Connecticut. Wallace had just spoken at Wesleyan University and my advisor's son was reading the newspaper. There was a picture of George Wallace on the front page, snarling at folks. My advisor's son for some reason didn't know that I was from Tennessee. And he said, 'You know, look at that,' pointing at the picture. 'The guy looks like a typical Southerner.'"

The Moral Responsibilities of Elected Officials

> "This moral issue. A moral issue comes from your heart in the first place. If I thought it was sinful and irreligious and immoral to separate myself socially and educationally from Nigra citizens, then I would commit a sin if I did so, I suppose. But I believe that separation is good for the Nigra citizen and the white citizen. And in their best interests. And if I do something that my heart tells me is good for both groups, there is not

anything that runs counter to any religion or any law of morality. It's not sinful."

> — George Wallace
> in a filmed interview in 1963

"I don't think he ever changed as far as his real feelings were concerned. I think he started articulating a different attitude for political purposes, but George didn't get converted and then reconverted. George just reverted to what he was all the time. Political expedience. He had to do it to get elected, and I lost a lot of respect for it because he paid a big price. When you sell your integrity for political expedience."

> — Frank Johnson
> in Jack Bass's
> *Taming the Storm*

The road that George Wallace traveled, as a young populist liberal in the 1940s, then as a racial reactionary in the early 60s, becoming the national "impresario of the politics of anger" in his presidential races, and finally ending as a moderate Southern Democrat in the 70s and 80s apologizing for his past sins, has been long and full of twists. But while Wallace proved himself the ultimate pragmatist, a politician able to move from getting elected as the most extreme segregationist in Alabama, to staying elected by depending on the mass votes of blacks, there are important questions raised by this life narrative.

Did officials elected during the period of violent Southern resistance to civil rights have a moral responsibility to peacefully move towards the inevitable changes that were in store for the South? While we reserve places of honor and respect for political leaders who are seen to have been "profiles in courage," standing up for their principles no matter what, many of those who choose to stand up in opposition to the majority will of their constituents, whether on moral principle or not, are soon defeated in elections and removed from office. In modern American politics, to be defeated and out of office is almost to cease to exist. There is no tradition of an opposition "shadow cabinet," defeated but waiting for its next chance to appeal to the public. And few would question the prevailing observation that it was next to impossible to be elected governor of Alabama in 1962 without advocating some support for the existing system of racial segregation. Andrew Young, having helped to lead the Southern Christian Leadership Conference's campaigns in Birmingham and Selma in the mid-1960s, remembers that: "It was almost impossible for decent white people, intelligent white people, to get elected in the South. You got elected by 'out-niggering' your opponent and so decent people refused to sink to that level of politics."

James MacGregor Burns, the biographer of Franklin Delano Roosevelt, in his study *Leadership* separates what he defines as *transactional* leadership — where leaders simply exchange their performance in office for the votes to keep them there — from *transforming* leadership, "a relationship of mutual stimulation and elevation that converts followers into leaders and may convert leaders into moral agents." What defines "leadership" is in the eye of the beholder. Few would question that FDR's New Deal helped transform the national partisan alignment for decades and created governmental policies that were associated long afterwards with his name. In Louisiana, Huey Long's platform of state populism (which differed from the platforms of other so-called Southern populists of his time in that he actually transformed it into law) also survived long after his death, still associated with his name. However one might define Wallace, he was clearly not a transformational leader. He did not initiate the issues that he was associated with, but, as so many observers of his political career say, he gave those issues "a voice."

Dan Carter, in his forthcoming biography of Wallace, calls him a mimetic orator, a leader who serves as a mirror to his audience. Such a leader does not seek to change the views or desires of his constituency, but acts as their spokesman and ignites the audience by playing on the emotions or issues that move them. In the South of the 1950s and 60s, for white voters who felt threatened by impending change, the political atmosphere was certainly charged and ripe for extreme rhetoric. Similarly, Merle Black notes that:

> "Wallace had a way of expressing in the vernacular of much of the working class and lower working class, exactly what they were feeling. They could hear their own thoughts coming back at them through Wallace. And by doing by this, he was saying, 'You've got a real grievance and I'm with you.'"

But the consequences of Wallace's ability to give to the people (or, at least, some of the people) that "voice" become much more problematic when you remember, as Black does, that while Wallace was governor "a lot of people really got hurt."

That Wallace chose to exploit and inflame the passions of the times is very clear. When his own attorney general warned him of increasing Klan violence and murders if he persisted in his public defiance of the federal government at every turn, Wallace replied, "Damn it, send the Justice Department. I'm gonna make 'em bring troops into this state." During his first term as governor, between 1962 and 1966, more people were killed in the civil rights struggle in Alabama — including four young girls in a Klan bombing of a black church in Birmingham — than anywhere else in the South, even in neighboring "bloody Mississippi."

Jack Bass and Walter DeVries, in their book *The Transformation of Southern Politics*, try to put Wallace's actions in perspective by looking at other Southern states at that time. What they find are other state leaders, who, while not actively advocating integration, were acting to douse the flames of violent resistance. Georgia's Governor, Carl Sanders, was "counseling racial moderation and compliance with the law." At almost the same time that Wallace was declaring "segregation forever" at his inaugural address, South Carolina's Governor, Ernest Hollings, was addressing his state legislature, informing them that they had run out of courts and should now obey orders to integrate "with dignity... and with law and order." Within a week, a young Harvey Gantt, years later the respected mayor of Charlotte, North Carolina, quietly enrolled at Clemson University — with state police providing security instead of blocking his way.

Another example is the path pursued by Judge Frank Johnson. Johnson, a hill country Republican, one of Wallace's closest friends at the University of Alabama Law School in the 1940s, aspired to a career in law. Years later, fate would cross their paths in Johnson's federal court- room. There, Wallace would seek to defend segregation (and further his own political career) while Johnson would rule to carry out the law. Using his power as a federal judge, Johnson struck down Alabama's segregation laws and ordered the registration of black voters and the integration of the state police — but at a personal cost. Wallace made him the brunt of his statewide campaign attacks, calling Johnson "an integrating, scalawagging, race-mixing, bald-faced liar" who needed a "barbed wire enema." And while Wallace rose to power in Alabama with this violent rhetoric in the early 1960s, Johnson lost friends, suf- fered the bombing of his mother's house, and grieved after his only son committed suicide.

Is politics all cynical calculation? How real are personal transformations in politics? George Wallace, says Tuskegee Institute political scientist Larry Hanks, was seen by African-Americans as "the arch stereotypical racist." But this "pragmatic racist" — pragmatic in the assumption that his stance was solely based on getting elected — as Hanks described him, has spent much of his later life seeking forgiveness and apologiz- ing for the wrong he once represented. He even received an honorary degree from the historic black Tuskegee Institute, an honor that was clearly important to him. Historian Linda Reed, like Dr. Hanks a native black Alabamian, stresses that for the African-American community in Alabama, Wallace's repenting was "a very real thing."

In telling Wallace's story, all questions about political calculation and core beliefs lead to the "turning" point in his political life, the only election in Alabama he ever lost. In 1958 the young Wallace was beaten by a more extreme segregationist candidate for governor. The consequences of the choice that he made that night, never to be "out-niggered again," was to remake himself into an apostle of racial hatred. In Robert Penn Warren's novel about power and politics and human need, *All the King's Men*, the character of Willie Stark/Huey Long, at first an idealist, experiences a similar realization of the need to "give 'em what they want to hear." On the verge of discovering that he's been taken for a sap, encouraged to run for office in order to split the "rural" vote to allow the "city boys" to take the governorship, he tries to tell Jack Burden, the cynical newsman covering his crumbling campaign, that the people need to hear the specifics of his programs, need to hear why what he proposes is best for them. Losing his patience, Burden cuts him off:

> "Yeah, I heard that speech. But they don't give a damn about that. Hell, make 'em cry, make 'em laugh, make 'em think you're their weak erring pal, or make 'em think you're God-Almighty. Or make 'em mad. Even mad at you. Just stir 'em up, it doesn't matter how or why, and they'll love you and come back for more. Pinch 'em in the soft place. They aren't alive, most of 'em, and haven't been alive in twenty years. Hell, their wives have lost their teeth and their shape, and likker won't set on their stomachs, and they don't believe in God, so it's up to you to give 'em something to stir 'em up and make 'em feel alive again. Just for half an hour. That's what they come for. Tell 'em anything. But for Sweet Jesus' sake don't try to improve their minds."

The great debate, in both Stark's career, as it may have been in Huey Long's actual career, becomes a question of means justifying the ends. Certainly both stood for something. One could make the case that Wallace stood for nothing besides a cynical political expediency. But just as Stark whispers to Burden, on his death-bed after being shot, that "it might have been all different Jack — you got to believe that," Wallace might have made different choices, perhaps used his power in different ways. Marshall Frady, in his biography of Wallace, quotes one Alabama political observer speculating how "Wallace and the state would have been entirely different if he had won that first time." But the facts — and the history — are that he did not win that race. And that he made the subsequent choices that he did. This film must grapple with those choices. It must seek to understand why George Wallace made the choices that he did and what his leadership meant, to friends and foes alike.

History of the Project

The initial idea for *Settin' the Woods on Fire: The Life and Times of George Wallace* began with producer Paul Stekler's work on the *Eyes on the Prize II* series in 1989. The original treatment for the *Eyes* program about Martin Luther King's last year, "The Promised Land, 1967-68," included a concluding section on the election of 1968 and the country's turn towards more conservative national politics. Archival research on the 1968 presidential campaign turned up reels of dramatic campaign material from Wallace's often frenzied and raucous campaign rallies.

Among the people interviewed on film for "The Promised Land" was Tom Turnipseed, the co-director of the 1968 national Wallace ballot-drive that successfully put George Wallace's name on the general election ballot as a third party candidate in all fifty states. Turnipseed, who in the years since had come full circle politically and run (unsuccessfully) for governor of South Carolina as a populist and a racial liberal, had been recommended by a number of the series scholars. His filmed interview, discussing Wallace's campaign in 1968 from the inside — Wallace's reactions to the huge crowds he was drawing, their explicit strategy and success in dealing with the issue of race through code terms, and conversations Turnipseed had had with Wallace supporters as he did advance work for the campaign — was extraordinary. The highlights included a description of an encounter that Turnipseed had with Wallace supporters at a club in rural Massachusetts — included in this proposal's script — that *Eyes* series writer Steve Fayer and series consulting producer Jon Else thought was one of the strongest stories filmed for the entire series.

Eventually, the 'Wallace/1968 Election' sequence, though powerful, was dropped to allow the film to fully focus on Dr. King and his immediate legacy — and Stekler began thinking about the possibilities of returning to George Wallace in a separate film. In his previous career as a professor of political science, Dr. Stekler's specialty had been Southern politics, with his main focus being the dynamics of change in the politics of the American South during the civil rights years. His dissertation focused on African-American politics in the South and the impact of the re-enfranchisement of the South's black population on the dynamics of the region's politics — and, in turn, the impact of the changing dynamics of Southern politics on the politics of the nation. Wallace's political career, and his political impact, were crucial parts of his work — and as film material, Wallace's story seemed a natural compliment to the history covered by *Eyes on the Prize*.

Soon after finishing his *Eyes* films, Stekler met with Dan Carter, who was working on a biography of Wallace. Having read and admired Dr. Carter's *Scottsboro: A Tragedy of the American South*, on the Scottsboro Boys case, Stekler approached him about doing a film on Wallace. Carter and Stekler talked about the need for such a film, particularly the need to explain Wallace's career and public appeal in the context of the white South, a focus rarely undertaken by recent documentary film work. This would involve an in-depth portrait of the politics and society that produced and shaped Wallace. They agreed to work together, a collaboration that eventually extended to doing some field work together in Alabama. Over the past two years, Dr. Carter shared a decade's worth of research that he had conducted for his upcoming biography, *The Politics of Rage*, including his notes, hundreds of transcribed interviews, an extensive newspaper and magazine clippings file, hundreds of photo-graphs (many obtained from private collections), and suggestions for other primary materials and sources, along with the drafts of his thousand page manuscript. His previous experience in advising film projects was helpful in advising us on characters who could provide compelling inter-views on film. Dr. Carter also opened doors to convince individuals, who had turned down interview requests for years in the past, to talk to us. Carter's and Stekler's early work together helped produce the successful Scripting grant for this project to the NEH. One measure of their collab-oration is that Dr. Carter's Wallace biography ends with a quote from Virginia Durr that was originally recorded during Paul Stekler's film proj-ect research in Montgomery — a quote that was shared with Carter. That quote now also ends the Wallace script.

During the NEH supported Scripting phase of the project, Stekler and his staff made eight separate research trips down South. These trips provided an opportunity to conduct a comprehensive review of the archival film and photograph collections at a number of Southern and national network archives. Well over a thousand network stories and locally shot film reels were found and catalogued. Copies were made of over forty hours of material, including film shot in all of Wallace's political campaigns (including campaign commercials from 1958 on) and official film spots shot while he was governor. A large number of pre-interviews were also conducted and transcribed. As material was collected, Steve Fayer and Paul Stekler began writing a draft script.

In March 1994, the entire scholar's board for the Wallace project met for three days at Emory University in Atlanta to watch the collected select reels of archival film and critique an interim sixty page Wallace film script in detail. The discussion was lively, spirited, and very positive. The representative of the NEH, who attended the sessions, described them as one of the best scholar's meetings that she had ever attended. Similar feelings were expressed by the advisors. The three day discus-sion was recorded, transcribed, and then used, along with the marked up scripts and numerous follow-up calls to the advisors, for a substan-tial script rewrite that is included in this grant application.

Production Schedule

Continued refining of the draft script and location research on *Settin' the Woods on Fire* will continue through the spring and summer of 1995. It is anticipated that the Production phase of the project will begin late this year. All the participant personnel and advisors for this film project proposal have been advised of the proposed schedule of activities. What follows is an outline of the Production and Post-Production process:

Fall 1995-Summer 1996:
Production on the film begins with location filming in Alabama. Additional film interviews will probably take place in central locations such as Atlanta, Washington, and New York.

Archival film research, in the network archives in New York and in the various Southern archives researched during the scripting phase, will be completed, with archival pulls marked and dubbed to video. It is anticipated that the schedule for production and archival collection will allow editing by the summer of 1996.

Summer 1996-Spring 1997:
The filmed interviews and location shots will be transferred to video, digitized, and loaded into an Avid editing system, along with the archival film. Editing will begin in the summer, with a rough cut anticipated for the fall. The advisory board will convene in Atlanta to review and critique the rough cut of the film in the early fall.

Once the edit is locked, early in 1997, the narration and the final score for the film will be recorded and sound editing, including period music, will commerce. Sound effects, dialogue tracks, music, and narration will be prepared for a final sound mix. The final locked digitized Avid visuals will be matched back to allow negative cutting to finish the project on film. A completed film, along with a master video dub for television broadcast, is anticipated in the spring of 1997.

Packaging for national broadcast on PBS will depend on the film's placement in the national schedule. Publicity and promotion will include long-lead press releases and special screenings at least three months prior to the PBS broadcast. It is possible that one of the PBS affiliates will act as a presenting station for the film. In Paul Stekler's current association with WETA-TV on the *Vote for Me: Politics in America* series, WETA is handling all national PR and is having great success in placing stories about the series, even though the PBS airdate is not until October 1996.

Key Personnel

Paul Stekler (Project Director, Producer, Co-Writer) has produced six hour-length documentaries dealing with subjects involving American history and politics, all of which have been broadcast nationally on public television. His last two films aired in 1992: *Last Stand at Little Bighorn*, a reexamination of the Battle of the Little Bighorn from both Native and white perspectives, co-written with Native-American novelist James Welch (and supported by an NEH grant), was broadcast as part of the series THE AMERICAN EXPERIENCE. It attracted a national television audience of six million viewers and won an Emmy Award. *Louisiana Boys: Raised on Politics*, a humorous, irreverent look at the Bayou State's politics, from the days of Huey Long up to today, co-produced with Louis Alvarez and Andrew Kolker, was broadcast as part of PBS's P.O.V. series and was awarded an Alfred I. duPont-Columbia University Award for Broadcast Journalism. Previously, Stekler co-produced two films (with Jacqueline Shearer) for *Eyes on the Prize II*, the acclaimed PBS series about the civil rights movement. "The Promised Land, 1967-68", focusing on Dr. Martin Luther King's Poor People's Campaign, his death, and Resurrection City, was nominated for two national Emmys. Critics described this film as "television so profound, it would justify 80 hours of prime time" and "the most moving, if not the best program in *Eyes on the Prize*." Stekler's earlier work consisted of two films about African-American politics in the modern American

South: *Hands That Picked Cotton: The Story of Black Politics in the Rural South*, which received a Gabriel Award and a nomination for best documentary feature film at the American Film Festival and *Among Brothers: Politics in New Orleans*, which won a Red Ribbon at the American Film Festival. He is currently finishing production on a series about American political culture, *Vote for Me: Politics in America*, that will be the centerpiece of PBS's election year programming in 1996.

Stekler has a doctorate in American politics. His dissertation was entitled "Black Politics in the New South." He later wrote academic articles on politics in the South and taught Southern politics for five years at Tulane University in New Orleans, where he was also a political consultant.

Steve Fayer (Writer) was the series writer for both *Eyes on the Prize* and *Eyes on the Prize II*, where he and Paul Stekler first worked together. He received an Emmy for his script "Mississippi: Is This America?", part of the first *Eyes* series. He was also the co-author (with Henry Hampton) of *Voices of Freedom*, a history of the civil rights movement that was named as one of the "notable books of the year" by the New York Times. Recent script credits include Series Writer for *The Great Depression*, an NEH-funded series of seven one-hour documentaries; *Malcolm X: Make It Plain*, a two-and-one-half hour special for THE AMERICAN EXPERIENCE; *After the Crash*, a one-hour documentary for THE AMERICAN EXPERIENCE; and *Frederick Douglass: When the Lion Wrote History*, a 90-minute documentary for PBS. He also served as Series Consultant for *America's War on Poverty*, five one-hour documentaries telecast January 1995 on PBS; for *Driving Passion*, a four-hour series on the history of the American automobile for Turner Broadcasting; and is currently Series Consultant for *Chicano: History of the Mexican American Civil Rights Movement*. Fayer is an honors graduate of the University of Pennsylvania, and a MacDowell Fellow. He has worked in film and television for more than thirty years.

Dan McCabe (Editor) has edited over twenty films for national public television broadcast. His most recent credits include editor and co-director on the hugely popular NEH-supported *Columbus and the Age of Discovery* series; editor and co-producer on WGBH's *Nixon* series (for which he was nominated for a national Emmy); editor and co-producer on the NEH-supported *Eisenhower* series on THE AMERICAN EXPERI-ENCE; and editor on WGBH's *Mexico* series. He also did additional edit-ing for the *Kennedy* series that aired on THE AMERICAN EXPERIENCE. He is currently finishing producing and editing two films for WGBH's *History of Rock and Roll* series.

John Grybowski (Archival Film Researcher) worked closely with Paul Stekler on his *Eyes on the Prize* films. Among his major contributions to the "The Promised Land" program was finding all of the existing film footage of Martin Luther King's 'Mountaintop Speech' (delivered the night before Dr. King's death), pieced together from five separate film archives. His experience at the NBC News Archives, based on seven years as an NBC film researcher, was extremely helpful in turning up important archival film, found in mislabeled or unmarked film cans. A freelance film and tape researcher since 1987, Mr. Grybowski has most recently worked on *America's War on Poverty*, *The Great Depression*, WGBH's *Nixon* series, and on two films for PBS's FRONTLINE series, in addition to his *Eyes on the Prize* work.

Robin Espinola (Associate Producer) has worked with Midnight Films for the last three years, most recently as an Associate Producer on the series *Vote for Me: Politics in America*. Before that, she worked on a number of national productions including *The Great Depression* and *Malcolm X: Make it Plain*.

While no specific cinematographer is set for the production of *Settin' the Woods on Fire*, it is anticipated that we will be working with some-one who has worked with Paul Stekler on his previous work. Jon Else

(*Yosemite: The Fate of Heaven, Eyes on the Prize*) shot Stekler's *Last Stand at Little Bighorn.* Michael Chin (*Eyes on the Prize II, Malcolm X: Make it Plain*) worked with Stekler on *Eyes II.* Buddy Squires (*The Civil War, Baseball*) has filmed several preliminary interviews for the Wallace project. Stekler has talked about the production of the film with each of them and given complimentary schedules; it is hoped that one of these cinematographers will film the bulk of the interviews and the location shooting for this project.

Humanities Advisors

The academic advisors for this film represent many of the best known and most respected scholars of the American South and of this historic period. They were chosen to represent a diversity of perspectives, specialties, and scholarly fields, covering both the South and a general overview of American politics and history. Between them, they have written thirty-eight books on various aspects of Southern history, politics, and identity, in addition to numerous articles and other scholarly publications.

Project Director Paul Stekler has worked closely with large boards of advisors in the past, both on the *Eyes on the Prize* series and on *Last Stand at Little Bighorn.* As in those previous projects, the academic advisors have been involved from the start, helping to frame the larger questions that the films addressed while also helping to locate both potential interviewees and useful historical materials. The attached script is the product of that collaboration. Our commitment to involving the advisors at every step of the production process remains unchanged. Our advisors are:

Dan Carter (chief advisor) is the Andrew W. Mellon Professor in the Humanities at Emory University in Atlanta, Georgia, the current President of the Southern Historical Association, and has written extensively on Southern history. He is best known for his book *Scottsboro:*

A Tragedy of the American South, about the case of the Scottsboro Boys, which won the Bancroft Prize in History. More recently, he wrote *When the War was Over: The Failure of Self-Reconstruction in the South, 1865-1867.* He has advised numerous film projects dealing with the American South, including *The American South Comes of Age*, a thirteen part, NEH funded series on the twentieth-century South — and he serves on the academic advisory committee for PBS's history series THE AMERICAN EXPERIENCE. He has been a member of the Board of Editors of *Southern Studies* and the *Journal of Southern History*.

Dr. Carter's new biography, *The Politics of Rage: George Wallace and His America*, will be published by Simon & Schuster later this year. Discussions between Dr. Carter and Paul Stekler about the possibilities of doing a film about George Wallace began in 1990. They have collaborated closely since then, sharing interviews, archival materials, and, at times, conducting location research together, during the period when Dr. Carter was finishing his Wallace biography and the film was in its development and scripting phase.

Note: Stekler goes on below to describe each of the advisors in detail as above for Dan Carter – to save space here I am deleting the descriptive paragraphs.

Jack Bass (advisor) is a Professor of Journalism at the University of Mississippi....
Merle Black (advisor) is the Asa G. Candler Professor of Politics and Government at Emory University ...
Alan Brinkley (advisor) is Professor of History at Columbia University, specializing in twentieth-century American political and intellectual history...
David Garrow (advisor) is the James Pinckney Harrison Visiting Professor of History at the College of William and Mary...
Virginia Van der Veer Hamilton (advisor) is Professor, University Scholar Emerita, and former Chairperson of the Department of History at the University of Alabama at Birmingham...

Lawrence Hanks (advisor) is the Dean for the office of Afro-American Affairs at Indiana University...

Gary Orren (advisor) is the Associate Director of the Joan Shorenstein Barone Center on the Press, Politics, and Public Policy at the John F. Kennedy School of Government at Harvard University...

John Shelton Reed (advisor) is the William Rand Kenan, Jr., Professor of Sociology and Adjunct Professor of American Studies at the University of North Carolina...

Linda Reed (advisor) is a historian with a joint appointment as an Associate Professor in the History Department and the Director of African American Studies Department at the University of Houston...

J. Mills Thornton (advisor) is the Richard Hudson Research Professor of History at the University of Michigan...

Filmography

It would seem impossible to make a film about the political history of this country in the 1960s without including George Wallace. A generation after he walked onto the national stage, he remains a major icon of the period. Just watching a few moments of archival film footage of Wallace flailing away in front of a huge crowd, denouncing the federal government or the civil rights movement or anti-war protesters, is enough to evoke the political passion of the times.

Indeed, Wallace pops up in many of the recent major public television documentaries covering this period, including *Eyes on the Prize, Making Sense of the Sixties*, and David Grubin's *LBJ*. In the past, Wallace has also appeared in programs dealing with broader American history — as in Bill Moyers' *A Walk Through the Twentieth Century* — and in programs focused more narrowly on the recent history of the South — as in South Carolina Educational Television's series *The American South Comes of Age*. But most of these films are focused on other stories and Wallace, and his supporters, rarely have more than a walk-on role.

WGBH's recent series of documentaries on American presidents (*The Kennedys, LBJ, Nixon*) provides a good illustration of this. The films are mostly biographies, the rise and fall of larger-than-life politicians or dynastic families. Thus, for example, Wallace turns up briefly in the third part of the four-hour *LBJ* film. In the immediate aftermath of the attack by Alabama State Police and sheriff's deputies on marchers in Selma, we see Wallace being invited up to the White House and given "the Johnson treatment." In a lovely three and a half minute sequence of back-and-forth cutting between two Johnson advisors who were present at the meeting, Richard Goodwin and Nicholas Katzenbach, Johnson's method of persuading Wallace to call out the Alabama National Guard to protect the marchers is brought to life. We hear Goodwin quote Johnson: "What do you want left behind? You want a great big marble monument that says: George Wallace - He Built. Or do you want a little scrawny pine lying there along that harsh bleachy soil that says: George Wallace - He Hated?" The narrator tells us that Wallace later said, "If I hadn't left when I did, he'd of had me coming out for civil rights." But that's it. Just those three plus minutes in a four hour film. There is no real mention of Wallace's impact on the national politics, or his presidential candidacy in 1968. The film, and everyone in it, revolves around its main character, Lyndon Johnson. It is not Wallace's story. And when one watches *The Kennedys* or *Nixon*, Wallace does not appear and is not mentioned at all in seven hours of film — this despite what Dan Carter — this project's chief academic advisor and author of a major new Wallace biography — writes in his attached supporting letter, saying that: "I do not believe Richard Nixon ever made a major decision on domestic issues without inserting George Wallace into the calculus of his political equations."

In *Eyes on the Prize*, Wallace turns up as a leader of the opposition to civil rights, standing in the door to bar black students at the University of Alabama and presiding as governor of Alabama during both the civil right movement's Birmingham campaign in 1963 and the 1965 campaign in Selma. But this is a movement history, the story of the civil rights struggle told by the people who made that movement happen. While other voices are heard — including several brief interview bites by an elderly and ill George Wallace, filmed in 1986 — again, this is not their story. There is, for instance, no examination of how George Wallace rose to power, of his impact on the North and on Richard Nixon's domestic agenda.

George Wallace is a major character in the famous Drew Associates film about the crisis over the integration of the University of Alabama in 1963. Recut and broadcast as *Kennedy vs. Wallace: A Crisis Up Close*, for the series THE AMERICAN EXPERIENCE, the film is mostly wonderful behind-the-scenes footage of both Wallace and the Kennedy brothers as they approach the famous standing-in-the-school-door standoff (and subsequent registration of two black students). This film, though, is only about a very brief period of the times to be covered by *Settin' the Woods on Fire: The Life and Times of George Wallace*, although we hope to be able to use some of the footage.

There have been two documentaries that primarily focus on George Wallace's life: *George Wallace: A Politician's Legacy*, a production of Alabama Public Television that first aired in Alabama in 1988, and a 1994 segment of Arts and Entertainment's 'Biography' series, *George Wallace: The Politics of Race*. The Alabama Public Television program was targeted largely for an Alabama audience and was never broadcast nationally by PBS. It covers every Wallace political campaign in great detail, but provides little historical context and few analytical perspectives. The Arts and Entertainment program, while covering much of Wallace's career, rushes through the story without great depth.

This proposed film project, *Settin' the Woods on Fire: The Life and Times of George Wallace*, offers an approach to both Wallace and the political history and legacy of his times that has not been attempted before. We will not only place George Wallace's life and political career into a much broader historical context, but will use the drama of his own rise in politics and his own political transformation into the national symbol of resistance to civil rights to illustrate the profound impact of racial politics in the 1960s on the subsequent national politics of the United States, to examine and attempt to understand the kind of public response that Wallace seemed to touch and mobilize, and to muse on the eternal question in democracies — the responsibility of leaders to lead people or to be led by them.

Visualization

The dramatic events surrounding the political career of George Wallace — and the larger history that he played a role in — lend themselves well to documentary film treatment. This period of history has already provided the basis for some of the most moving and memorable documentary film work of our time, particularly in the *Eyes on the Prize* series. The visualization of the Wallace story involves a similar use of materials — archival film footage and photographs, interviews with participants in the history and with historians of the period, location film shooting, and the use of personal memoirs, letters, and journals.

The sources that can be used for this film are particularly rich. Governor Wallace's political career was well documented by the national news media after his arrival onto the national political stage, dating to his 1963 stand in the schoolhouse door. Well over a thousand separate network stories involving Wallace between 1963 and 1972 have been found and catalogued at the NBC, CBS, Sherman Grinberg/ABC, Fox/Movietone, and WTN archives. Searches through hand written story cards have already begun to turn up film of Wallace before his election as governor of Alabama attracted national attention. One such find is black and white footage of Wallace's 1959 confrontation with Judge Frank Johnson over the release of local voting registration lists, Wallace's first filmed attacks on the federal government and on his former law school friend, all the while surrounded by a state press pack eager for soundbites.

The initial treasure hunt for additional non-network archival film has also begun to turn up amazing footage that has not been used to document

Wallace's life before. The film and videotape archives of the local television affiliates in Montgomery, Birmingham, and Tuscaloosa, Alabama, are particularly good sources. Among the gems found there have been campaign films compiled for Governor Jim Folsom (themselves a wonderful record of oldtime, stump speaking Southern political rallies in the 1940s and 50s) that include Wallace, looking like a teenager, delivering a blistering 1954 attack on Folsom's high-class, conservative opponents. The local stations also saved the best record of Lurleen Wallace's stump speeches — short, calm speeches she had memorized, delivered in the middle of frenzied crowds, anticipating her husband's speeches that always followed — in her successful 1966 gubernatorial campaign.

The most valuable Alabama archive examined during the research phase of this project was a collection of materials that the Wallace family had donated to the University of Alabama in Birmingham. The materials included much of Wallace's private correspondence, including many of the letters and telegrams sent to him in the 1960s and 70s. The telegrams sent to him after his "stand in the schoolhouse door" that are quoted in the draft script in this proposal were part of this collection.

Over a hundred reels of film and two-inch videotapes were also included in these materials, most of it later copied for the archives of Alabama Public Television (but almost none of it used for their own Wallace documentary). The visual material is priceless. It includes complete filmed Wallace campaign speeches and rally coverage from his 1958 and 1962 statewide campaigns. There are also his first state television commercials (including 1962 staged scenes shot in barbershops, beauty parlors, and at truckstops, where people ask each other: "Isn't everyone voting for Wallace?") and his presidential ads (including ads of Wallace and his whole family, shot in 1964 while they were all campaigning in Indiana's presidential primary, and Paul Harvey hosted half-hour specials in 1968). The best material, over forty hours in total, has been copied and catalogued by the Wallace film project staff and now available for our film. This, along with new material discovered at a number of Southern archives (such as the University of South Carolina's Movietone Newsreel collection, the Mississippi Department of Archives and History in Jackson, Mississippi, the University of Georgia's WFS collection, and the Birmingham Public Library), will allow Wallace's political career to be illustrated as never before.

There is no shortage of still photographs of Governor Wallace either. Private collections and public archives, though, are turning up more material. Dan Carter, for instance, recently found a series of photos of Wallace as a college student at the University of Alabama, including five stills of Wallace competing in a campus pie-eating contest, before, during (on his knees on stage, his face buried in the pie), and after, his broad smile partially obscured by the pie filling. Wallace's career as a state and college bantamweight boxer in the 1930s is also recorded in still photos. When Wallace's second wife Cornelia describes an old photograph of Wallace, pummeling a bloody opponent, using it as a key to understanding his personality, we have the still.

Location photography will also play a key role in the film, especially in establishing Alabama as a setting for Wallace's politics. Filming at the exact locations of tumultuous past events — where Wallace stood in the schoolhouse door, looking up at the window of the hotel room where he vowed never to be "outniggered again," standing by the side of the church in Birmingham where four young girls were killed in a 1963 bomb blast — places where quiet now reigns can be very evocative. Match-dissolves, matching contemporary locations to those same locations, filmed thirty and forty years in old archival footage, is another possible use of live modern cinematography. One could film a series of driving perspectives, past a number of rural Southern scenes, establishing the South — or Alabama — as a place, then match-dissolving while driving into a particular town, a place where Wallace is seen speaking to a political crowd in the late 1950s or early 60s. We have already found old black and white Wallace campaign footage, shot from cars driving into county courthouse square rallies, and matched it to those same roads and locations in Alabama today. That very use of a match-dissolve scene setting can be seen in the very first sequence in the draft script that follows.

A large list of potential interviewees for *Settin' the Woods on Fire: The Life and Times of George Wallace* is included later in this proposal. While the list of compelling and colorful storytellers for this narrative is long, an important question to be confronted during production is whether a filmed interview with Governor Wallace should also be conducted. Wallace was interviewed at length for both *Eyes on the Prize* and the Alabama Public Television documentary, both in 1980s. Wallace has been in bad health, in great pain, and deaf for years. He is easily distracted and nearly impossible to understand when he talks. Since the 1980s, his health has steadily declined. A recent Connie Chung *Eye-to-Eye* magazine piece on Wallace was painful to watch. Dr. Stekler's observations of Wallace in Alabama indicate that the potential for interviewing him is extremely low. Our goal is to use the older interviews of Wallace, filmed throughout his life, in order to have Wallace's "voice" at the center of the film. That said, it is our goal to visit with Governor Wallace, before major production begins, for a final evaluation.

The Life and Times of George Wallace will have a five-act structure:

- Act I: **"A Real Do-Gooder"** explores the roots of Wallace's political drive, from his youth in rural Alabama through his rise as a racially moderate populist at the state level, and culminating in a crushing defeat for the governorship in 1958. Losing to a more extreme segregationist candidate, Wallace vows he will never be "outniggered" again.

- Act II: In **"A Kind of Meanness in the Air,"** Wallace's re-creation of himself as an ardent segregationist pays off. Winning the Alabama governorship in 1962, his first term is marked by a series of bloody civil rights confrontations that cement Wallace's control of state politics and bring him national recognition.

- Act III: Wallace's move onto the national political stage is the focus of **"You Gonna See the Whole Country Southernized."** Running for president as a third-party candidate in 1968,

Wallace capitalizes on the urban and campus disorders of the late 1960s, winning ten million votes and turning the election into a referendum on "law and order."

- Act IV: **"Somebody's Gonna Get George Sooner or Later"** follows Wallace, bolstered by his '68 campaign and determined to take the presidency in 1972. He returns to Alabama to rebuild his financial and political strength and following an overtly racist campaign, is elected governor again. By 1971, his stand against school busing and for "states rights" has placed him in a Gallup Poll as one of "the men Americans most admired." The Wallace presidential campaign is in full swing by 1972. President Nixon fears another Wallace third-party candidacy and searches for ways to stop it. Opponents in the Democratic Party are in disarray. But Wallace's campaign — and his national aspirations — come to an abrupt end at a shopping mall in Laurel, Maryland, when he is shot by a would-be assassin.

- Act V: **Epilogue: "We All Worship in the Same Church"**. The ailing Wallace holds on to political office, in the 1970's and 80s — with the support of Alabama's black voters. In this closing chapter, the film re-examines Wallace's impact on American politics, and the choices that he made, and the choices the American people made in this critical period in our history.

Prologue: Race and Class

We fade up on a filmed interview with the late William Bradford Huie, journalist, novelist, eighth generation Alabamian:

"Poor white men have always got a very dirty deal in the South. In the slave days, blacks — slaves — looked down on poor white men. And well-off white men looked down on landless white men in the way that well-off people in India look down on their poor people. So I have sympathy for the poor white man in the South because I've had a poor white man looked up to me and he said — 'Mr. Huie, if I ain't better than a damned nigger what the hell am I better'n of?' Now it's all well enough to dismiss — except Aristotle wrote two thousand years ago that every man *yearns* to be recognized for something."

Crossfade to moving shot — a country road in southeastern Alabama, early morning, and superimpose MAIN TITLES:

SETTIN' THE WOODS ON FIRE:
THE LIFE AND TIMES OF GEORGE WALLACE

On the car radio, through static, we hear Hank Williams:

"Comb your hair, and paint and powder
You act proud and I'll act prouder
You sing loud and I'll sing louder
Tonight, they're settin' the woods on fire."

The sun flashes on the broken window of an abandoned cabin, flares through tree branches — as we continue to move past the Alabama woods of the title song — tall oak, black gum, and pine; past woodsmoke curling from brick chimneys, old Fords rusting into the earth of side yards, old wringer washing machines and ice boxes, rusted Dr. Pepper and R.C. Cola signs in stamped metal; painted barnboard advertising for snuff and chewing tobacco, the vices of the rural poor. We overtake a storm of wind-blown cotton issuing from a truck laden with bales and move past a modest, white church, small and square-shouldered out in the distance of a plowed field.

The road leads into a small town, a county seat — the courthouse in the distance. Drawing near to the almost deserted square, we lose the Hank

Williams lyric and begin to hear the sounds of a large milling crowd. The picture slowly match-dissolves into black-and-white footage of the same courthouse square, three decades earlier, filled with hundreds of spectators fanning themselves in the hot sun as they listen to a young political candidate. The newsreel lens moves in to study the speaker in close-up, his head tilted to the side.

It is a young George Wallace in shirtsleeves, his narrow tie askew, running a cupped hand over dark, oiled hair as he moves along the planks of a flatbed truck, his hands jabbing at some invisible opponent, his whole body giving off an athlete's energy as he speaks:

> "They call us peapickers, and peckerwoods and lint heads and rednecks."

Solemn men in bib overalls contemplate the speaker.

> "Let them call us rednecks, if they mean our necks might be red from a good honest day's toil in the summer sun. But there's two things about those people who call us that. Number one, they won't work, and number two, their hair's so long their necks wouldn't get red anyway."

The hands are out of the overalls now, applauding. A young woman stares as if transfixed. Another smiles behind her hand, shyly.

> "They sit up there in their ivory towers and they put us down 'cause we don't do what they want us to do."

Again, the crowd roars its approval. From somewhere in the back, where young men lounge against pickup trucks, we hear a rebel yell.

As Wallace's voice begins to fade in the square of more than thirty years ago, our present day witnesses begin to comment on the man and his message, and on themes that will run through the film. We hear first from an old man speaking in the measured accent of rural Alabama:

"All those little farmhouses stuck way out in the woods, they all had a TV set you know. When those folks saw Wallace on there standin' up to those big-city slick-hair boys, that wasn't just him talkin'. That was *them* on there."

An older man in a worn suit, Seymore Trammell, once Wallace's closest aide:

"He had that gut feeling that he could determine just exactly what was really on the minds of the people, what the hot buttons were that needed to be pushed. He wanted power — and he was willing to sacrifice everything, everything and anybody that was in his way. He was ready to abandon family, friend, political philosophy."

Jack Bass, a Southern journalist:

"Liberals. Coddled criminals. Welfare cheats. Federal bureaucrats. In the 1960s, George Wallace denounced them all. To many people in that era of rapid social change, his message seemed like the retrograde rantings of a political throwback. But now his issues are the issues of the today."

Andrew Young, aide to Martin Luther King, Jr.:

"We were trying to prove that there was a new South where blacks and whites could work together. But when George Wallace began to attract followers in Michigan, in Wisconsin, places that we thought were liberal, then it was clearly a threat. The threat that we would lose what we had gained. The threat of violence."

White-haired Virginia Durr, a longtime Alabama activist:

"The violence. It was there already. George didn't create that. He ran on it. It was the people of Alabama that gave him the power to do what he did. It was people like me, who was raised a racist. It was all of us that created this situation. But I can't blame George for something that everybody in Alabama was guilty of."

Opening narration:
George Wallace. In the 1960s and 70s, he symbolized resistance to civil rights in this country. He was the man who stood in the schoolhouse door — to keep blacks out. The man who said — "segregation now, segregation tomorrow, and segregation forever." He was known for the furious energy of his attacks against people he called hippies, civil rights agitators, welfare recipients, beatniks, pointy-headed intellectuals, anti-war protesters, communists, and street thugs who he said had "turned to rape and murder cause they didn't get enough broccoli when they were little boys." He transcended his southern roots to speak for a national backlash against civil rights, for the alienated and angry "silent majority." He was four times Governor of Alabama, four times a candidate for President of the United States.

In his early years, he was condemned by southern conservatives as too liberal. In his first years in power, he was feared by many — as a racist demagogue.

It is the conclusion of those who study American politics that George Wallace could never have been President. But there are millions of other Americans who believed then — and believe now — that George Wallace told truths that other politicians were afraid to speak. And that he deserved the highest office in the land.

His career demonstrates beyond any doubt that racism was never the exclusive property of any particular American region. And that the prejudices and polarization blamed on the South were alive and at work in the entire country. George Wallace's story is Shakespearean in its omens and portents, and in its march toward tragic conclusion. And at its center is a quicksilver character who continues to puzzle even those who were closest to him.

Did he believe in his positions on race? Or was he simply a cynical opportunist in love more with power than with principle? Was he at heart a good man gone wrong and later redeemed? Or is the real truth about George Wallace locked in the snarling, sneering speeches of his political heyday — when Americans had little doubt about who he was and what he stood for? Many believed he changed us as a nation — changed our political loyalties, the structure of our major political parties, and in a real sense, helped "southernize America." In a democracy, there is a need to search for answers, and for standards by which to judge those who seek to lead us. Perhaps if we come to understand George Wallace, we will better understand ourselves — and the forces that were let loose in our nation during his life in politics.

Wallace biographer Dan Carter:

> "Long before journalists and pundits coined the term 'silent majority,' Wallace understood that there might not be a majority, but there were millions of Americans who felt that nobody was paying any attention to them, that nobody cared about their frustrations. No respectable spokesman from the right was ever willing to acknowledge ties or links to his ideas. But no, I don't think we can make any sense of American politics in the 1960s and 1970s — and afterwards — without understanding the critical role George Wallace played in transforming those politics."

Note: In the following pages, deleted here, Stekler continues the detailed treatment for the five acts of the film.

List of Potential Interviewees

The following is a partial list of potential film interviewees. It was compiled from our pre-interviews, conducted during the Research and Scripting phase of the project, along with the suggestions of the project's advisory board. Dr. Dan Carter, who has interviewed most of the people listed here for his Wallace biography, was particularly helpful in advising the project on potential interviews. Not everyone contacted to-date is listed here and the list of potential film interviewees will continue to grow. Some of the people ultimately included in the film will not be famous, well-known, or well connected, but will be plain people, black and white, whose lives were touched or effected by Wallace.

Ralph Adams: A college friend who ran a boarding house where Wallace often slept. A life-long friend, Wallace appointed him as a university president in the 1960s.

Brandt Ayers: Editor of the *Anniston, Alabama Star*.

Melvin Bailey: Sheriff of Jefferson County, Alabama, during the Southern Christian Leadership Conference's Birmingham desegregation campaign in 1963.

Winton "Red" Blount: Postmaster General in the Nixon administration and an important member of the Republican Party in Alabama. Now a developer in Montgomery.

Albert Brewer: Former Wallace political ally as his Speaker of the Alabama House, Lt. Governor under his wife, and later Governor after her death. He lost for reelection in a bitter race against Wallace in 1970.

Note: Stekler spends three more pages listing 38 more possible interviewees as above – eliminated here for space. Also eliminated: A "Selected Bibliography," "Resumes of Key Personnel and Humanities Advisors and Letters of Commitment," *and* "Selected Reviews of Previous Work by Paul Stekler."

National Endowment for the Humanities
BUDGET FORM

OMB No. 3136-0086
Expires: 6/30/95

Project Director

Paul Stekler

Applicant Organization

Filmmakers' Collaborative

If this is a revised budget, indicate the NEH application/grant number:

Requested Grant Period

From Nov. 1995 to March 1997

This three-column budget has been developed for the convenience of those applicants who wish to identify the project costs that will be charged to NEH funds and those that will be cost shared. FOR NEH PURPOSES, THE ONLY COLUMN THAT NEEDS TO BE COMPLETED IS COLUMN C. The method of cost computation should clearly indicate how the total charge for each budget item was determined. If more space is needed for any budget category, please follow the budget format on a separate sheet of paper.

When the requested grant period is eighteen months or longer, separate budgets for each twelve-month period of the project must be completed on duplicated copies of the budget form.

SECTION A — budget detail for the period from Nov. 1995 to March 1997

1. Salaries and Wages

Provide the names and titles of principal project personnel. For support staff, include the title of each position and indicate in parentheses the number of persons who will be employed in that capacity. For persons employed on an academic year basis, but separately pay salary charges for work done outside the academic year.

name/title of position	No.	Method of cost computation (see sample)	NEH Funds (a)	Cost Sharing (b)	Total (c)
See attached budget			$	$	$
detail pages that					
follow.					
		SUBTOTAL	$	$	$ 169,000

2. Fringe Benefits

If more than one rate is used, list each rate and salary base

rate	salary base	(a)	(b)	(c)
12.65 % of	$ 169,000	$	$	$ 21,379
% of	$			
	SUBTOTAL	$	$	$ 21,379

3. Consultant Fees

Include payments for professional and technical consultants and honoraria.

name or type of consultant	no. of days on project	daily rate of compensation	(a)	(b)	(c)
See attached budget		$	$	$	$
detail pages.		$			
		$			
		$			
		$			
	SUBTOTAL		$	$	$ 14,000

NIH Budget Form   Page 2

4. Travel

See attached budget detail

SUBTOTAL ... $ 39,885

5. Supplies and Materials

See attached budget detail

SUBTOTAL ... $ 27,000

6. Services

See attached budget detail

SUBTOTAL ... $ 423,435

NEH Budget Form

Page 3

7. Other Costs

Include participants stipends and room and board, equipment purchases, and other items not previously listed. Please note that "miscellaneous" and "contingency" are not acceptable budget categories. Refer to the budget instructions for the restriction on the purchase of permanent equipment.

Item	Basis/method of cost computation	NEH Funds (a)	Cost Sharing (b)	Total (c)
See attached		$	$	$
budget detail				
	SUBTOTAL	$	$	$ 261,500

8. Total Direct Costs (add subtotals of items 1 through 7)

	NEH Funds	Cost Sharing	Total
	$	$	$ 948,022

9. Indirect Costs (This budget item applies only to institutional applicants.)

If indirect costs are to be charged to this project, check the appropriate box below and provide the information requested. Refer to the budget instructions for explanations of these options.

☐ Current indirect cost rate(s) have/have been negotiated with a federal agency. (Complete items A and B.)

☐ Indirect cost proposal has been submitted to a federal agency but not yet negotiated. Indicate the name of the agency in item A and show proposed rate(s) and base(s) and the amount(s) of indirect costs in item B.)

☐ Indirect cost proposal will be sent to NEH if application is funded. (Provide an estimate in item B of the rate that will be used and indicate the base against which it will be charged and the amount of indirect costs.)

☐ Applicant chooses to use a rate not to exceed 10% of direct costs, less distorting items, up to a maximum charge of $5,000. (Under item B, enter the proposed rate, the base against which the rate will be charged, and the computation of indirect costs or $5,000, whichever sum is less.)

A. _____   _____
   Name of federal agency   Date of agreement

B.

Rate(s)		Base(s)	NEH Funds (a)	Cost Sharing (b)	Total (c)
____ % of	$ _____		$	$	$
____ % of	$ _____		$	$	$
		TOTAL INDIRECT COSTS	$	$	$ 0

10. Total Project Costs (direct and indirect) for Budget Period

NEH Funds	Cost Sharing	Total
$ 948,022	$	$ 948,022

NEH Budget Form   Page 4

SECTION B — Summary Budget and Project Funding

SUMMARY BUDGET

Transfer from section A the total costs (column c) for each category of project expense. When the proposed grant period is eighteen months or longer, project expenses for each twelve-month period are to be listed separately and totaled in the last column of the summary budget. For projects that will run less than eighteen months, only the last column of the summary budget should be completed.

Budget Categories	First Year *(a)*	Second Year *(b)*	Third Year *(c)*	TOTAL COSTS FOR ENTIRE GRANT PERIOD
1. Salaries and Wages	$	$	$	= $ 169,000
2. Fringe Benefits				= 21,379
3. Consultant Fees				= 14,000
4. Travel				= 39,885
5. Supplies and Materials				= 27,800
6. Services				= 423,458
7. Other Costs				= 252,500
8. Total Direct Costs (Items 1-7)	$	$	$	= 948,022
9. Indirect Costs	$	$	$	= -0-
10. Total Project Costs (Direct & Indirect)	$	$	$	= $948,022

PROJECT FUNDING FOR ENTIRE GRANT PERIOD

Requested from NEH		Cost Sharing	
Outright	$ 948,022	Cash Contributions	$
Federal Matching	$	In-Kind Contributions	$
		Project Income	$
TOTAL NEH FUNDING	$ 948,022	TOTAL COST SHARING	$ -0-

Total Project Funding (NEH Funds + Cost Sharing) = $ 948,022

Indicate the amount of outright and/or federal matching funds that is requested from the Endowment.

Indicate the amount of cash contributions that will be made by the applicant or third parties as support project expenses that appear in the budget. Include in this amount third party cash gifts that will be raised to release federal matching funds. (Consult the program guidelines for information on cost-sharing requirements.)

Occasionally, in-kind (noncash) contributions from third parties are included in a project budget as cost sharing, e.g., the value of services or equipment that is donated to the project free of charge. If this is the case, the total value of in-kind contributions should be indicated.

When a project will generate income that will be used during the grant period to support expenses listed in the budget, indicate the amount of income that will be expended on budgeted project activities.

Total Project Funding should equal Total Project Costs.

Institutional Grant Administrator

Complete the information requested below when a revised budget is submitted. Block 11 of the application cover sheet instructions contains a description of the functions of the institutional grant administrator. The signature of this person indicates approval of the budget submission and the agreement of the organization to cost share project expenses at the level indicated under "Project Funding."

John Sinkerman, Secretary-Treasurer
(Name and Title (please type or print)

(signature)

Telephone (617) 643-3071

Date *Feb. 20, 1995*

SETTIN' THE WOODS ON FIRE:
The Life And Times Of George Wallace

Date: MARCH 3, 1995

BUDGET SUMMARY

Salaries and Wages	169,000
Fringe Benefits	21,379
Consultant Fees	14,000
Travel	39,885
Supplies and Materials	27,800
Services	423,458
Other Costs	252,500
TOTAL BUDGET COSTS	**948,022**

SALARIES AND WAGES

	Quantity	Cost	Total
Staff:			
Producer	52 wks	1450	75400
Associate Prod.	52 wks	1000	52000
Office Manager	52 wks	800	41600
TOTAL SALARIES & WAGES			**169000**

BENEFITS

Benefits (FICA, FUTA, SUTA)	@ 12.65% of salaries		21379
TOTAL BENEFITS			**21379**

CONSULTANT FEES

Scholars	11 persons, 40 days	350	14000
TOTAL CONSULTANTS			**14000**

TRAVEL

Production -- 5 trips, 5 people, 28 days			
Airfare	25 flights	500	12500
Hotel/Per Diem	5 people for 28 days	100	14000
Ground -- Van Rental	28 days	75	2100
Excess Bags			600
Consultant Meeting to view Rough Cuts in Atlanta -- 11 advisors, 2 days			
Consultants	11 flights	500	5500
Hotel/Per Diem	11 people for 2 days	100	2200
Ground -- Van Rental	3 days	75	225
Archival Material Travel			
Airfare	2 flights	500	1000
Hotel/Per Diem	5 days	100	500
Ground -- Car Rental	5 days	40	200
Narrator Travel to New York			
Airfare	1 flight	500	500
Hotel/Per Diem	2 days	250	500
Ground			60
TOTAL TRAVEL			**39885**

SUPPLIES AND MATERIALS

Office Supplies	12 mos.	400	4800
Production Supplies:			
Film Stock	150 rolls	100	15000

Sound stock	100 tapes		10	1000
Beta Videotapes	50 tapes		40	2000
Post-Production Supplies				2000
Video 1" stock				1500
Video dubs				1500

TOTAL SUPPLIES AND MATERIALS 27800

SERVICES

Archival Footage & Photos:

Researcher	12 wks	1100		13200
Archival access	12 wks	1600		19200
Archival film repro	25 hrs.	400		10000
Archival Photo repro	50	30		1500
Animation				
Stand rental	20 hrs.	150		3000

Freelance Personnel:

Writer	15 wks	2500		37500
Editor	32 wks	1700		54400
Asst. Editor	34 wks	800		27200
Sound Editor	4 wks	1300		5200
Cinematographer	28 days	500		14000
Asst. Camera	28 days	275		7700
Sound Recordist	28 days	350		9800

Production Equipment:

Camera Rental	28 days	350		9800
Sound Rental	28 days	250		7000
Expendables				600
Special Equip.				1000
Misc.				1000

Office expenses:

Office rent	12 mos.	1400		16800
Computers	3 for 12 mos.	150		5400
Telephones	12 mos.	700		8400
Xerox	12 mos.	300		3600
Postage Freight	12 mos.	300		3600
Fax machine	12 mos	50		600
Misc.				1000
Accounting				3000
Legal				3000
Non-Profit Admin.				
(inc. all insurance, prod., E&O)				36000

Lab/Tape Expenses (shooting film,
  digitizing for Avid editing, finishing in film):
Process, Transfer to

Video & Synching	60000 ft	.30		18000
Avid rental	8 mos.	4000		32000
Avid maintenance				3500
Negative Cutting				4000

1st answer print	4400 ft	.73	3213
Corrected answer prints	8800	.41	3608
Interpositive	4400	1.1	4840
Opticals			4000
Fades/Dissolves			600
Check print	4400	.35	1540
Release print	4400	.195	858
Film-to-1" tape	16 hrs.	550	8800
Sound:			
Narration/Voice-over recording			4000
Sound Effects			1000
Sound Mix	30 hrs	500	15000
Original Music Composition & Recording			15000

TOTAL SERVICES   423458

OTHER

Narrator			10000
Voice Overs			2500
Rights:			
Music (period recordings)			25000
Archival Film Footage	76 min	@ 2500	190000
PR Budget			25000

TOTAL OTHER   252500

TOTAL DIRECT COSTS (1-7) $ 948,022

BRIEF BIBLIOGRAPHY

What follows is a short list of helpful fundraising resources.
For a much more extensive list that is updated regularly, come to my
Web site:
www.warshawski.com

BOOKS ON FUNDRAISING

Bergan, H. *Where the Money Is*. Arlington, Virginia: BioGuide Press.

Broce, Thomas E. *Fund Raising: The Guide to Raising Money from Private Sources*. Oklahoma City: Univ of Oklahoma Press.

Cones, John W. *43 Ways to Finance Your Feature Film*. Carbondale, Illinois: Southern Illinois University Press.

Corporate 500: The Directory of Corporate Philanthropy. San Francisco: Public Management Institute.

Environmental Grantmaking Foundations. Rochester, NY: Environmental Data Research Institute.

Flanagan, Joan. *The Grass Roots Fundraising Book: How to Raise Money in Your Community*, and *Successful Fundraising*. Chicago: Contemporary Books.

Golden, Susan and Shrader, Alan. *Secrets of Successful Grantsmanship: A Guerrilla Guide to Raising Money*. San Francisco: Jossey-Bass.

Hillman, Howard. *The Art of Winning Corporate Grants*. New York: The Vanguard Press.

Klein, Kim. *Fundraising for Social Change.* Berkeley: Chardon Press.

Kuniholm, R. *Maximum Gifts by Return Mail: An Expert Tells How to Write Highly Profitable Fund Raising Letters.* Detroit: The Taft Group.

Lautman, Kay Partney and Goldstein, Henry. *Dear Friend: Mastering the Art of Direct Mail Fund Raising.* Detroit: The Taft Group.

Revolution in the Mailbox. Berkeley: Strathmoor Press.

Robinson, Andy. *Grassroots Grants: An Activist's Guide to Proposal Writing.* San Francisco: Jossey-Bass.

Rosso, Henry A. *Achieving Excellence in Fund Raising: A Comprehensive Guide to Principles, Strategies, and Methods.* San Francisco: Jossey-Bass.

Scribner, Susan M. *How to Ask for Money Without Fainting.* Long Beach, California: Scribner & Associates.

Seymour, Harold. *Designs for Fundraising.* New York: McGraw.

Successful Fundraising. Chicago: Contemporary Books.

Warshawski, Morrie. *The Fundraising Houseparty: How to Get Charitable Donations from Individuals in a Houseparty Setting.* Ann Arbor: Morrie Warshawski.

Warwick, Allen & Stein. *Fundraising on the Internet.* New York: John Wiley & Sons.

Warwick, Mal. *Raising Money by Mail.* Berkeley: Strathmoor Press.

White,Virginia. *Grants and Grant Proposals That Have Succeeded.* New York: PUB.

Why Fund Media: Stories from the Field. Washington, DC: Council on Foundations.

BOOKS ON INDEPENDENT FILM / VIDEO

Baumgarten, Farber & Fleischer. *Producing, Financing and Distributing Film.* New York: Limelight Editions.

Bowser, Kathryn. *AIVF Guide to International Film and Video Festivals.* New York: AIVF.

Buzzell, Linda. *How to Make it in Hollywood.* New York: Harper Perennial.

Cones, John W. *The Feature Film Distribution Deal: A Critical Analysis of the Single Most Important Film Industry Agreement.* Carbondale, Illinois: Southern Illinois Univ. Press.

Cones, John W. *Film Finance & Distribution: A Dictionary of Terms.* New York: Silman-James Press.

Durie, John; Pham, Annika; Watson, Neil. *Marketing & Selling Your Film Around the World: A Guide for Independent Filmmakers.* New York: Silman-James Press.

Hampe, Barry. *Making Documentary Films and Reality Videos: A Practical Guide to Planning, Filming, and Editing Documentaries of Real Events.* New York: Owlet Press.

Harmon, Renee. *The Beginning Filmmaker's Business Guide.* New York: Walker and Company.

Hedlund, Patricia. *A Bread Crumb Trail Through The PBS Jungle: The Independent Producer's Survival Guide.* Pine Mountain, California: Dendrite Forest Books.

Laloggia, Nicole and Wurmfeld, Eden. *IFP/West Independent Filmmaker's Manual.* New York: Focal Press.

Lee, John J. *The Producer's Business Handbook.* New York: Focal Press.

Levison, Louise. *Filmmakers and Financing: Business Plans for Independents.* Burlington, Massachusetts: Butterworth-Heinemann.

Litwak, Mark. *Dealmaking in the Film and Television Industry: From Negotiations to Final Contracts.* New York: Silman-James Press.

Lukk, Tiiu. *Movie Marketing: Opening the Picture and Giving It Legs.* New York: Silman James Press.

Mackaman, Julie. *Filmmaker's Resource: The Watson-Guptill Guide to Workshops, Conferences & Markets, Academic Programs, Residential & Artist-In-Residence Programs.* New York: Watson-Guptill.

Mayer, Michael. *The Film Industries: Practical Business/Legal Problems in Production, Distribution, and Exhibition.* New York: Hastings House.

Mookis, Ioannis (ed.) *AIVF Self-Distribution Tool Kit.* New York: AIVF.

Moore, Schuyler M. *The Biz: The Basic Business, Legal and Financial Aspects of the Film Industry.* New York: Silman-James Press.

Pierson, John. Spike, Mike, Slackers & Dykes: *A Guided Tour Across a Decade of American Independent Cinema.* New York: Miramax Books.

Resnik, Gail and Trost, Scott. *All You Need to Know About the Movie and TV Business.* New York: Fireside Press.

Singleton, Ralph R. *Film Scheduling/ Film Budgeting Workbook: Do It Yourself Guide.* Berkeley: Lone Eagle Press.

Squire, Jason E. (ed.) *The Movie Business Book*, second edition. New York: Fireside/Simon & Schuster.

Vachon, Christine and Edelstein, David. *Shooting to Kill: How an Independent Producer Blasts Through the Barriers to Make Movies That Matter.* London: Avon Books.

Vogel, Harold L. *Entertainment Industry Economics: A Guide for Financial Analysis.* Cambridge, England: Cambridge University Press.

Warshawski, Morrie (ed.). *The Next Step: Distributing Independent Films And Videos.* New York: AIVF

Wiese, Michael. *Film and Video Budgets.* Studio City, California: MWP.

Wiese, Michael. *Film and Video Marketing.* Studio City, California: MWP.

Wiese, Michael. *Producer to Producer: Insider Tips for Entertainment Media.* Studio City, California: MWP.

Wiese, Michael. *The Independent Film and Videomakers Guide.* Studio City, California: MWP.

HELPFUL WEB SITES

ACTION WITHOUT BORDERS
www.idealist.org

ARTIST HELP NETWORK
www.artisthelpnetwork.com

ASSOCIATION OF FUNDRAISING PROFESSIONALS
www.afpnet.org

THE CHRONICLE OF PHILANTHROPY
www.philanthropy.com

THE COUNCIL ON FOUNDATIONS
www.cof.org

THE FOUNDATION CENTER
www.fdncenter.org

FOUNDATIONS ON LINE
www.foundations.org

ENTERTAINMENT LAW RESOURCES FOR FILM, TV, AND MULTIMEDIA
PRODUCERS
www.marklitwak.com

GRANTSNET/ U.S. DEPARTMENT OF HEALTH AND HUMAN SERVICES
www.hhs.gov/grantsnet

MEDIA RIGHTS.ORG
www.mediarights.org

MORRIE WARSHAWSKI'S FUNDRAISING BIBLIOGRAPHY
www.warshawski.com

NATIONAL ALLIANCE FOR MEDIA ARTS AND CULTURE
www.namac.org

NATIONAL ASSEMBLY OF STATE ARTS AGENCIES
www.nasaa-arts.org

NEW YORK FOUNDATION FOR THE ARTS/ INTERACTIVE
www.nyfa.org

WHY FUND MEDIA
www.fundfilm.org

PHOTO: PAUL THACKER

MORRIE WARSHAWSKI is a consultant, facilitator, and writer who specializes in helping nonprofit organizations on issues of strategic long-range planning. Warshawski received a BA and MA in English from the University of Southern California, and attended the Graduate Writers' Workshop in Iowa. His work in the nonprofit sector includes serving as the Executive Director of three arts organizations (Bay Area Video Coalition, Northwest Media Project, Portland Dance Theater) and, since 1986, as a consultant to a wide variety of clients including The National Endowment for the Arts, National Assembly of State Arts Agencies, St. Louis Black Repertory Company, John D. & Catherine T. MacArthur Foundation, PEW Charitable Trusts, San Francisco Museum of Modern Art, Yerba Buena Center for the Arts, and many others.

As a writer, Warshawski's works have appeared in many journals and newspapers (*Emmy Magazine, Grantmakers in the Arts Newsletter, Los Angeles Times, Modern Poetry Studies, Parenting, San Francisco Examiner* and many others). In addition to *Shaking the Money Tree*, his books include: *The Fundraising Houseparty, The Next Step,* and *A State Arts Agency Planning Toolkit.*

Warshawski does consult with independent filmmakers (in person and by phone) on issues of career development and fundraising plans. A full description of his "Initial Consultation" requirements and costs (along with upcoming travel plans for workshops and seminars) can be found on his Web site:

www.warshawski.com

If you are a filmmaker who wants assistance with fundraising, please be aware that Warshawski does not do any fundraising or any grantwriting.

DIGITAL FILMMAKING 101
An Essential Guide to Producing Low-Budget Movies

Dale Newton and John Gaspard

The Butch Cassidy and the Sundance Kid of do-it-yourself filmmaking are back! Filmmakers Dale Newton and John Gaspard, co-authors of the classic how-to independent filmmaking manual *Persistence of Vision*, have written a new handbook for the digital age. *Digital Filmmaking 101* is your all-bases-covered guide to producing and shooting your own digital video films. It covers both technical and creative advice, from keys to writing a good script, to casting and location-securing, to lighting and low-budget visual effects. Also includes detailed information about how to shoot with digital cameras and how to use this new technology to your full advantage.

As indie veterans who have produced and directed successful independent films, Gaspard and Newton are masters at achieving high-quality results for amazingly low production costs. They'll show you how to turn financial constraints into your creative advantage — and how to get the maximum mileage out of your production budget. You'll be amazed at the ways you can save money —and even get some things for free — without sacrificing any of your final product's quality.

"These guys don't seem to have missed a thing when it comes to how to make a digital movie for peanuts. It's a helpful and funny guide for beginners and professionals alike."
> — Jonathan Demme
> Academy Award-Winning Director
> *Silence of the Lambs*

Dale Newton and John Gaspard, who hail from Minneapolis, Minnesota, have produced three ultra-low-budget, feature-length movies and have lived to tell the tales.

$24.95, 283 pages
Order # 17RLS | ISBN: 0-941188-33-7

SETTING UP YOUR SHOTS
Great Camera Moves Every Filmmaker Should Know

Jeremy Vineyard

Written in straightforward, non-technical language and laid out in a nonlinear format with self-contained chapters for quick, on-the-set reference, *Setting Up Your Shots* is like a Swiss army knife for filmmakers! Using examples from over 140 popular films, this book provides detailed descriptions of more than 100 camera setups, angles, and techniques — in an easy-to-use horizontal "wide-screen" format.

Setting Up Your Shots is an excellent primer for beginning filmmakers and students of film theory, as well as a handy guide for working filmmakers. If you are a director, a storyboard artist, or an animator, use this book. It is the culmination of hundreds of hours of research.

Contains 150 references to the great shots from your favorite films, including *2001: A Space Odyssey*, *Blue Velvet*, *The Matrix*, *The Usual Suspects*, and *Vertigo*.

"Perfect for any film enthusiast looking for the secrets behind creating film. Because of its simplicity of design and straightforward storyboards, *Setting Up Your Shots* is destined to be mandatory reading at film schools throughout the world."
— Ross Otterman, *Directed By Magazine*

Jeremy Vineyard is a director and screenwriter who moved to Los Angeles in 1997 to pursue a feature filmmaking career. He has several spec scripts in development.

$19.95, 132 pages
Order # 8RLS
ISBN: 0-941188-73-6

DIRECTING & VISUALIZATION

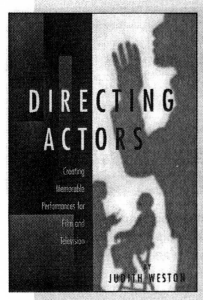

DIRECTING ACTORS
Creating Memorable Performances for Film & Television

Judith Weston

Over 20,000 Sold!

Directing film or television is a high-stakes occupation. It captures your full attention at every moment, calling on you to commit every resource and stretch yourself to the limit. It's the white-water rafting of entertainment jobs. But for many directors, the excitement they feel about a new project tightens into anxiety when it comes to working with actors.

This book provides a method for establishing creative, collaborative relationships with actors, getting the most out of rehearsals, troubleshooting poor performances, giving briefer directions, and much more. It addresses what actors want from a director, what directors do wrong, and constructively analyzes the director-actor relationship.

"Judith Weston is an extraordinarily gifted teacher."
> — David Chase, Emmy Award-Winning Writer,
> Director, and Producer
> *The Sopranos, Northern Exposure, I'll Fly Away*

"I believe that working with Judith's ideas and principles has been the most useful time I've spent preparing for my work. I think that if Judith's book were mandatory reading for all directors, the quality of the director-actor process would be transformed, and better drama would result."
> — John Patterson, Director
> *The Practice, Law and Order, Profiler*

Judith Weston was a professional actor for twenty years and has taught Acting for Directors for over a decade.

$26.95, 314 pages
Order # 4RLS
ISBN: 0-941188-24-8

SCRIPT PARTNERS
What Makes Film and TV Writing Teams Work

Claudia Johnson & Matt Stevens
Foreword by Marshall Brickman

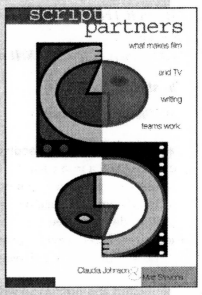

Many of the most important and successful films and television shows of the past and the present have been written by script partners, from Billy Wilder's legendary collaborations with Charles Brackett and I.A.L. Diamond to the Coen Brothers' collaboration today; yet, no serious study exists of this unique and important process. Of the more than two hundred books about screenplay and television writing available today, not one focuses on collaborative writing.

This book brings together the experience, knowledge, techniques, and wisdom of many of our most successful writing teams for film and television. It examines the role and the importance of collaboration, then illuminates the process of collaborative screenwriting itself: its unique assets, from the partners' complementary strengths to the mysterious but often-mentioned "third voice" that occurs during collaborative writing; why and how they choose each other; the myriad ways that different teams work; how teams create their ideas, choose projects, develop character, story, and structure, write scenes, dialogue, draft the screenplay, rewrite, and how they manage and maintain their creative relationship. At its deepest level, that's what collaborative screenwriting is about: human relationships.

Includes interviews with such successful collaborators as Andrew Reich & Ted Cohen (*Friends*), Jim Taylor (*Election, About Schmidt*), Marshall Brickman (*Annie Hall, Manhattan*), Scott Alexander & Larry Karaszewski (*The People vs. Larry Flynt, Ed Wood*), and Larry Gelbart (*M*A*S*H*).

Claudia Johnson is the author of *Stifled Laughter*, nominated for the Pulitzer Prize, and *Crafting Short Screenplays That Connect*. Matt Stevens is a Los Angeles-based writer/producer who has sold both fiction and documentary projects. Two of their co-written scripts were recent finalists for the Sundance Screenwriters Lab.

$22.95, 300 pages
Order # 104RLS | ISBN: 0-941188-75-2 | **Available February 2003**

THE SCRIPT-SELLING GAME
A Hollywood Insider's Look at Getting Your Script Sold and Produced

Kathie Fong Yoneda

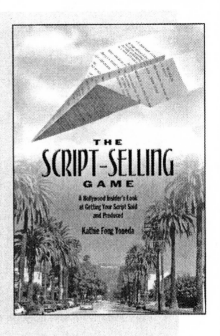

There are really only two types of people in Hollywood: those who sit around wearing black clothes in smoky coffee shops, complaining they can't get their scripts past the studio gates... and then there are the players. The ones with the hot scripts. The ones crackling with energy. The ones with knowledge.

Players understand that their success in Hollywood is not based on luck or nepotism; it's the result of understanding how Hollywood really works.

The Script-Selling Game brings together over 25 years of experience from an entertainment professional who shows you how to prepare your script, pitch it, meet the moguls, talk the talk, and make the deal. It's a must for both novice and veteran screenwriters.

"Super-concise, systematic, real-world advice on the practical aspects of screenwriting and mastering Hollywood from a professional. This book will save you time, embarrassment, and frustration and will give you an extra edge in taking on the studio system."
> — Christopher Vogler, Author, *The Writer's Journey: Mythic Structure for Writers*, Seminar Leader, former Story Consultant with Fox 2000

"I've been extremely fortunate to have Kathie's insightful advice and constructive criticism on my screenplays. She has been a valued mentor to me. Now, through this wonderful book, she can be your mentor, as well."
> — Pamela Wallace, Academy Award Co-Winner, Best Writing, Screenplay Written Directly for the Screen, *Witness*

Kathie Fong Yoneda is an industry veteran, currently under contract to Paramount TV in their Longform Division, and an independent script consultant whose clientele includes several award-winning writers. Kathie also conducts workshops based on *The Script-Selling Game* in the U.S. and Europe.

$14.95, 196 pages | Order # 100RLS | ISBN: 0-941188-44-2

FILM DIRECTING: CINEMATIC MOTION
A Workshop for Staging Scenes

Steven D. Katz

With this practical guide to common production problems encountered when staging and blocking film scenes directors can better develop a sense of what is the right solution for any given situation. Includes discussions of scheduling, staging without dialogue, staging in confined spaces, actor and camera choreography, sequence shots, and much more — with hundreds of storyboards and diagrams.

Some of the staging examples are technically simple, others require substantial choreography. The underlying assumption for all is that the filmmaker wants to explore the dramatic potential of the camera to the fullest, within the day's shooting schedule.

Contains illuminating interviews with these well-known professionals, commenting on the practical aspects of production: director John Sayles (*Eight Men Out, Lone Star*), cinematographer Allen Daviau (*ET, Hearts of Atlantis*), visual effects expert Van Ling (*Doctor Doolittle, Not Another Teen Movie*), art director Harold Michelson (*Catch-22, Terms of Endearment*), producer Ralph Singleton (*Clear and Present Danger, Juwanna Mann*), and key grip Dusty Smith (*Rounders, Cop Land*).

"The art of staging movies scenes hasn't been written about very extensively, so the best way to learn is by watching others at work. *Film Directing: Cinematic Motion* provides a better idea with complete illustrated staging techniques and storyboards."
　　　　　　　　　　— *Millimeter Magazine*

Steven D. Katz is a writer/filmmaker. His work has appeared on *Saturday Night Live*, in feature films, and in numerous film festivals around the world. He is also the author of *Film Directing: Shot by Shot*.

$24.95, 294 pages
Order # 6RLS | ISBN: 0-941188-14-0

THE PERFECT PITCH
How to Sell Yourself and Your Movie Idea to Hollywood

Ken Rotcop as told to James Shea

A good pitch can mean the difference between seeing your name on a lucrative studio contract or a form rejection letter. It's a well-known industry fact that film executives typically devote about two minutes of their attention to directors and screenwriters who bring them their ideas hoping for a deal. Can you capture their attention and pique their interest in the time it takes to order a latte at Starbucks? Your future as a successful screenwriter or director may depend on it.

Author Ken Rotcop writes from a unique perspective — he's made hundreds of pitches himself as a screenwriter and producer and heard many more as creative director of four studios. Using personal examples of successes and failures, Rotcop shows you how to walk the tightrope of a pitch meeting without falling off. Which attention-grabbing strategies can make a studio head put down his daily horoscope and listen to you? Once you've got his attention, how can you "reel him in" and get him excited about your idea? What if you forget what you were going to say? What if you make a faux pas? Does "no" always mean "no" in the language of movie deals?

Rotcop discusses these situations and others, as well as how to best present yourself and your idea, how and when to do "on-the-spot" pitching, and how to recognize and capitalize on future opportunities.

"Forget about snappy dialogue, characterization and plot. It's the pitch that gets a script read and a movie deal done. If it were not for Ken Rotcop, most new writers would be out of the loop."
— John Lippman, *Wall St Journal*

Ken Rotcop produces Pitchmart™, Hollywood's biggest screenplay pitch event.

$16.95, 156 pages
Order # 14RLS | ISBN: 0-941188-31-0

ORDER FORM

MICHAEL WIESE PRODUCTIONS
11288 VENTURA BLVD., # 621
STUDIO CITY, CA 91604
E-MAIL: MWPSALES@MWP.COM
WEB SITE: WWW.MWP.COM

WRITE OR FAX FOR A FREE CATALOG

PLEASE SEND ME THE FOLLOWING BOOKS:

TITLE	ORDER NUMBER (#RLS _____)	AMOUNT
_____	_____	_____
_____	_____	_____
_____	_____	_____
_____	_____	_____
_____	_____	_____
	SHIPPING	_____
	CALIFORNIA TAX (8.00%)	_____
	TOTAL ENCLOSED	_____

PLEASE MAKE CHECK OR MONEY ORDER PAYABLE TO:

MICHAEL WIESE PRODUCTIONS

(CHECK ONE) ____ MASTERCARD ____ VISA ____ AMEX

CREDIT CARD NUMBER _____

EXPIRATION DATE _____

CARDHOLDER'S NAME _____

CARDHOLDER'S SIGNATURE _____

SHIP TO:

NAME _____

ADDRESS _____

CITY _____ STATE _____ ZIP _____

COUNTRY _____ TELEPHONE _____